LOVER SPOUSE

DOUGLAS WEISS, PH.D.

Lover Spouse
Copyright © 2019 by Douglas Weiss

Requests for information:
Discovery Press
heart2heart@xc.org
719-278-3708

All Rights reserved
Printed in the United States of America
ISBN #978-1-881292-40-1

No portion of this material may be reproduced in any
form or by any means without written permission of
the author.

Cover and Interior Design by Janelle Evangelides
Edited by: Carolyn Mader

Contents

Introduction

Every once in a while, you hear or read something, and it changes the whole way you think or feel about something. That is the goal of the book *Lover-Spouse*—to totally shift the way you think, feel, and behave in your marriage.

Now don't worry, I'm not sitting on a rock somewhere here in Colorado philosophizing on how to have great marriage. Like you, I've read marriage book after marriage book that are well written but don't really seem to add much to my daily life with my spouse. *Lover-Spouse* is a book that can shift everything in your marriage on a daily basis. I'm sharing with you the crème de la crème of ideas and paradigm thinking that has been helping Christian marriages for decades.

I'm not just an author, I'm actually a Christian psychologist who, every week for more than thirty years, has been resuscitating marriages. Every week couples fly in to my office in Colorado Springs and do intensive counseling for five days.

I've been in the ICU, if you will, of Christian marriages for decades. Every Monday in my office I hear the horror stories of a marriage about to die. I hear about infidelity at every level, porn, lying, withholding love and sex for years, and falling out of love. That's my typical Monday. However, more often that's not my Friday. By Friday, the couple likes or love each other and has a concrete plan to rebuild their marriage.

I've seen Christians fight for their marriages with new tools and new ideas. The lover-spouse idea has totally transformed lives again and again. I've seen marriages reinvigorated and reconnected as couples move into making their goal to be a lover-spouse. This paradigm shift changed how they thought, felt, and behaved in their marriage. No longer were they playing by the rules of keeping score or measuring themselves by their spouse's effort. Instead, they were free to be the best lover-spouse they could be in the marriage.

I want to be the first to welcome you to the exciting and fun world of being a lover-spouse.

The Paradigm Process

The wedding day is one of the most beautiful, emotional, expensive, orchestrated days of our life. Family members from both sides fly in, drive in, wear their best clothes, and happily navigate the rigors of the day's events.

They congregate at a set time, watch the groomsmen, and groom stand at the front. The classic tune "Here Comes the Bride" plays and then the most beautiful bride comes walking down the aisle. The pastor monologues for a while as we all wait for the pronouncement of, "I now pronounce you man and wife. You may now kiss the bride."

At that magical moment the two become one and we refer to them thereafter as husband and wife. We wait around for them as they take hundreds of pictures. We eat a great meal. We hang out with family and generally have a great time at the wedding.

The couple starts their new life as husband and wife. Usually they travel to a honeymoon to start their new life. Some of you are old enough to remember a radio personality named Paul Harvey and at this moment he would say, "And now the rest of the story."

The rest of this chapter is all about the paradigm-based thoughts and behaviors both the husband and wife have created for themselves as individuals as they move toward the wedding day. As we unravel the creation of these paradigms, I think you'll be able to see why so many couples have struggled, even as Christians, with marriage.

I know it's puzzling to us as Christians who love Jesus, love our spouse, are dedicated to His word, and desire to walk in His spirit, yet divorce is a common theme in our community. We need to dive into the paradigm process to expose the seeds of problematic thinking and believing that can cause a couple to have a challenging marriage.

I want to give you a little context on who I am and what I've been doing professionally for more than

thirty years. I'm a Christian counselor, psychologist, author, and speaker. For more than thirty years I've been counseling couples full time. I see Christian couples from every denomination, color, culture, life stage, and socioeconomic situation. For decades, couples have flown in to do intensives with me and my team at Heart to Heart Counseling Center located in Colorado Springs.

I evaluate the couples on multiple levels including their strengths, weaknesses, and spiritual, social, emotional, sexual, and environmental factors. Then I take time to evaluate the husband and wife separately going over their family of origin, sexual histories, etc. By the end of Monday, I have a pretty clear picture of the marriage and the individual issues that may be contributing to the marital strife, whether that be addictions, intimacy anorexia, sexual abuse or even personality disorders.

The rest of the week we address the marital and intimacy issues, provide the couple with tools to rebuild a successful marriage and create a long-term plan for the couple to live happily ever after—if they work the plan.

During this weekly process, after seeing so many couples I get an insight that can only come through time and experience. These couples open their hearts to me and expose what they actually think and truly believe about marriage. These marriage paradigms they've collected and created are often at the core of how they operate in a marriage.

These paradigms or ideas may be very biblical or very unbiblical. These paradigms may be very healthy or unhealthy, self-serving or giving. Whatever the paradigm, the paradigm has power. In Proverbs 23: 7, it says "As a man thinketh in his heart, so is he."

I can tell you as a Christian psychologist this scripture is so true. The paradigm you collected and created will be how you behave in your marriage. These paradigms create the framework or worldview you have of marriage, your role in marriage, and your expectations of your spouse in marriage. Your paradigm affects how you wake up and greet your spouse (in tolerance or celebration). Your paradigm determines who gets the other a cup of coffee, cooks meals, cleans up, creates wealth, pays bills, initiates sex and creates romance and so on. You can see how powerful paradigms can be in the way you believe and behave in your life.

{ *The paradigm you collected and created will be how you behave in your marriage.* }

However, rarely has anyone sat you and your spouse down and said, "let's go through your paradigm about your marriage." It's my experience that the paradigms are the roots that create the fruits in your marriage. For better or worse you'll cling to a known paradigm regardless if it's healthy or unhealthy if that paradigm isn't exposed and thought through differently.

In my thirty years of experience if a person's paradigm of marriage is more functional than relational, this in and of itself can create havoc in ten to twenty years of marriage. The lover-spouse paradigm is a relational paradigm that keeps both of you continuing to aim at staying a lover.

Creating a Paradigm

I wish that creating a paradigm was a simple process. It's not as simple as someone reading something in a book and that's how they created a paradigm. Oh no, far from it. Paradigms are collected, exposed and created—some over time, some by a one-time exposure, some through repeated good or bad experiences.

Let's begin by first looking at the bride. She may have come from a family with a great dad who regularly spoke life into her by stating things like, "You're awesome, smart, beautiful, capable, you can do anything." She experienced a man who praised well and often. She'll not only be secure and confident, she might also then generalize that all men are great at praising.

Generalizing is something all of us do in our life. After all, it's the only life experience we have so we draw conclusions as we go along. If you were a child and your neighbor had a mean German Shepherd, you would most likely believe (wholeheartedly, I might add) "All German Shepherd's are mean." This isn't true. We all generalize as a path to creating paradigms in all areas of our lives.

In a healthy family, one woman was raised as a person not an object. Her voice was heard, and she was respected. Again, she'll generalize that she'll be heard and respected. After all this is her life experience so believing this generalization would be normal.

Growing up, she might have heard her mother talk negatively about sex and how she dreaded it and thought it was a 'curse of wives.' If she absorbed this idea about sex, she might be challenged when it comes to sex. This would be an example of generalization based on a "trusted source." The bride's mother is a great influence in many ways. The daughter trusts her mother. So, the daughter could easily absorb the idea about sex being a curse. The daughter could easily create ideas surrounding this paradigm that could last a lifetime.

Her mother might have worked as a professional and attended every one of the daughter's important events, so she ultimately felt loved by her mom. This future bride has been collecting paradigms her whole life as to what the role of a woman is in marriage. By the time she walks down the aisle, she has ideas or paradigms about everything from who takes out the garbage, pays the bills, initiates sex, wants romance after marriage, has attitudes toward men and the role he has and doesn't have in her life, to who does or doesn't value the roles friends and parents play in their lives and so on.

The husband has also been collecting, experiencing, and creating paradigms. He might have grown up with a great mom. She stayed home, had dinner consistently on the table at 5 p.m., but was always busy cleaning and never really engaged much with him. He felt more managed than related to and his mom never asked him how he felt or what he thought about much. He had a list of chores and if these were done, he was praised and told he was a 'good boy.'

His dad might not have been very spiritual but tolerated going to church. He worked hard at work, which meant that he didn't do housework when he was home. He controlled the money since he earned it. He loved his wife but would put her down and make fun of her in public. Dad was always right, and the Bible told him he was ruler over mom. His dad had a stash of porn, which the son found, and this became his sex education since he never heard a word about sex from mom or dad. He learned some team concepts from being involved in sports and also witnessed other marriages, in which he picked up an idea or two about the roles of men and women in marriage.

I want to stop here and say neither of these people were aware they were absorbing ideas toward their future marriage. They grew up with the paradigm of their families. Some paradigms they accepted, others they flat rejected. However, the paradigms of your mother and father's marriage can be the most influential paradigms you bring to the wedding day. The consistent exposure to your parent's ideas about marriage is the "sauce" you were daily marinated in for at least two decades.

This marinating can soak deep into the soul and can put you in a place that you never even question the ideas or paradigms. The belief is what empowers these paradigms and is why you behave in the way you do in your marriage.

Not all marinating is bad. You might have seen raw courage, faith, and discipline in your parent's marriage. However, even in a strong marriage one, two or three paradigms can exist that you need to expose, challenge or even change to accommodate your marriage. Your marriage has bonded two beings from different paradigms, some of which might not be the best for your marriage.

> *The consistent exposure to your parent's ideas about marriage is the "sauce" you were daily marinated in for at least two decades.*

The bride and groom's experiences outside their family—neighbors, church members, pastors, friends, and other families all contributed to their paradigms in marriage as well. Their teachers, coaches, peers, and professors all had a comment or two that they also shared about the opposite sex and how to treat them. So, the paradigms we believe can come from anywhere. Television, the media, movies, the Internet, and social media all influence what we think, feel, and "believe" about marriage. This is why 2 Peter 2: 7-8 states that Lot was tormented in his righteous soul by the lawless deeds he saw and heard.

Our paradigms come from what we have seen or heard over the course of our life up to our wedding day. I think that is why Proverbs 4:23 tells us that above all else to "guard our heart for everything you do flows from it."

> { *Our paradigms come from what we have seen or heard over the course of our life up to our wedding day.* }

All of our lives we're collecting challenges and changing our paradigms. I encourage you to walk through that process throughout the rest of this book. Be thoughtful to evaluate your paradigms and the fruit of these paradigms and challenges. Look carefully at what you need to change and grow to be an awesome lover-spouse.

The Paradigm Problem

When someone creates a paradigm and questions it, that's one thing. However, when someone creates a paradigm and believes it with their heart, that becomes a whole other matter. As I said earlier, Proverbs 23: 7 states, "As a man thinks in his heart, so is he."

The heart is where we believe. The Bible says, "If you declare with your mouth that, 'Jesus is Lord,' and believe that in your heart that God raised him from the dead, you will be saved" (Romans 10:9). The heart is actually the most powerful thing we possess. When we believe something in our heart, then our mind, will, and emotions fully support this belief.

For example, for whatever reason if someone really believes they're worthless, they'll behave in worthless ways regardless of God's love, or their parent's and spouse's love. If someone believes they're worthy of love, they'll not accept disrespect or behavior toward them in a less than worthy way. More than anything, what we truly believe in our heart influences our behavior.

{ *When we believe something in our heart, then our mind, will, and emotions fully support this belief.* }

Our beliefs are the fuel for every paradigm you currently believe in all areas of your life. When you believe your paradigm, it grows and grows whether it's true or not. However, when you stop believing a paradigm it dies, often instantly. I remember clearly as if it was yesterday when Lisa rolled over in bed years after we were married and said, "I really love you."

I can't explain it but at that moment I really "believed" her. Once I believed her, all the previous paradigms instantly vanished. I can't tell you how many thousands of times I've seen that when someone believes a new paradigm, all the old ideas almost instantly disappear.

It's like when we really believe we are forgiven of all sin (past, present and future) by Christ and we fully let that in our hearts, we are changed. The past is gone, grace is real, and we become different.

I've counseled gorgeous, smart women who believed they were unattractive and unlovable. I've also counseled men who were millionaires and billionaires and believed they're unlovable and worthless. Facts are not necessarily when someone believes something in their heart.

Remember from history there was a time around the Christopher Columbus era that everyone thought the world was flat. They not only thought it, they believed it with their heart (paradigm). The church and political leaders of that day would persecute those who thought the world was round. Today we think this is ridiculous.

However, as a Christian psychologist, I can tell you that many a husband and wife fully think and believe in their paradigm of marriage or the role of the husband or wife with all their heart—regardless of facts or futility.

Personality and Paradigm

Your personality will also be key in your creating of paradigms for your role, your spouse's role in marriage, and for the marriage itself. We're delightfully human, and as such, we like to measure ourselves by our strengths not our weaknesses. As we create our role for ourselves in marriage, we often create a role we would naturally be good at that would require little dying to ourselves, and even less absolute dependence on the Holy Spirit to be able to maintain.

I am talking in generalizations of course. I'm sure there's a soul that says, "here is my weakest areas, I want to die to myself and serve you daily so I can become like Christ. I want to have all my flaws exposed in my marriage so I can repent often and become a better Christ-like person." If this is you, great. However, most of us like to live on our strengths not our weaknesses.

Jane is a very Godly woman and reads her Bible and prays daily, so she's a good wife. Jane is naturally organized and clean, so she's a good wife if things are clean and organized. Jane never gossips, so she's a good wife. Jane is naturally thin but exercises four times a week with her girlfriend. She has not "let herself go," so she's a good wife.

Trevor, Jane's husband, has a good work ethic and continually advances at the company he works for. Trevor is a good husband because he works hard. Trevor was raised by a handyman and can fix most things around the house. He's a good husband because he can do most things that need to be done around the house, saving the family money. Trevor is spiritually strong, reads his Bible daily, and makes sure he prays with Jane almost daily.

Both Jane and Trevor, with their self-created paradigms they've both bought into, believe they're great Christian spouses. What's interesting is they're on the brink of divorce as they sit in my office.

Jane fully believes she's a good spouse because she is Godly, keeps a clean home, and has stayed physically-fit and attractive. Trevor believes he's a good spouse because he provides well, fixes things, and prays regularly with Jane. They both randomly picked their strengths, created a paradigm of what constitutes "a good spouse" based on their personal strengths, and kept the focus on those strengths.

They created a friendship more than a lovership. Secretly, Jane is fuming at Trevor. He controls all the money, acts like God to her and the children, and can't ever share a true emotion or admit when he's wrong. Trevor is equally disappointed. He hasn't felt sexually desired for their entire marriage. He feels unappreciated for working hard at work and home. He feels so unloved because Jane rarely touches him unless its during sex.

The paradigm problem is when you so deeply believe you're a "good spouse" by measuring yourself by your own rules and roles you created in your mind, which may not have anything to do with the real needs or desires of your spouse.

When you created the paradigm of the good spouse, and you believed it in your heart, you're often close-minded and closed-hearted when given feedback that your paradigm might not be true, or it might not be working. You could easily become like the intolerant leaders of Christopher Columbus's day. So don't persecute your spouse, the pastor, friend or another that is trying to help you and challenge you.

When you tightly hold onto a paradigm and believe it's true, facts are irrelevant. You'll persist in your paradigm of the "good spouse" until you're all the way into divorce. Sadly, over the years I've counseled both men and women so committed to being good and right that they actually murdered a real marriage to hold to their paradigm.

Had this couple been open-hearted to a new paradigm of "lovership" instead of "good spouse," the marriage could've survived. In the following chapters I'll explain the lovership paradigm. However, before we leave the paradigm problem, I want to list out several paradigms that have been challenging for Christian couples to work through to become lovers again and have kept them chained to being good spouses.

When we believe we're good spouses and create rules and roles for ourselves or for our spouse, we can stay extremely stuck. We delved into Jane and Trevor's rules for themselves but what we didn't touch upon yet is the rules and roles that Jane and Trevor had for each other.

> { *When we believe we're good spouses and create rules and roles for ourselves or for our spouse, we can stay extremely stuck.* }

Jane grew up with an entrepreneur dad who became successful in a couple of businesses. Part of Jane's dad's processing about a new business venture was to talk to his wife about it and get her advice. Once the parents agreed their dad would share his new business idea with the children (and mom present), and everyone got to share ideas about the new business.

Jane's unspoken expectation for Trevor was that her husband would share his ideas, his heart, and adventure with his wife. Such a gesture signifies respect to Jane. Jane's dad was demonstrative with gifts of flowers, chocolate, cards and self-made/creative things for Jane's mom. Jane's other unspoken expectation for her husband would be he'll treasure her by buying her gifts and doing special things for her. Jane wasn't aware she was creating rules or roles for her future husband, but she was. She didn't tell Trevor that these were his rules or measures, so Jane stayed disappointed.

Trevor had a great mom. She praised every little thing he did. If he cleaned his room and put toys away, it was a big deal. He generalized that women praise you when you do things. A rule for his future wife was being laid in his heart. Trevor's mom was really affectionate—hugs and kisses were abundant for Trevor, which meant another expectation for his wife to be affectionate was being laid in Trevor's heart.

While both Jane and Trevor were performing excellently according to their own rules, they were drastically failing the rules and roles of their spouse. I wish Jane and Trevor were the exception, but honestly, this situation is so typical in challenging marriages.

As we move from being a good spouse by our own rules and move toward a lovership with our spouse, we can identify unhelpful paradigms and move toward pathways of loving our spouse in ways that actually work.

Dangerous Paradigms

I mentioned I'd share some of the top paradigms I see couples have that aren't helpful for their marriage. As I go through these, you might identify with one you're holding onto. That's great if you can see a problematic paradigm. We can't change what we can't see.

1. Marriage is between a man and a woman.

This is by far the most dangerous paradigm for a Christian marriage. This is 100% a secular idea and will ruin the foundation of your marriage. Marriage is between God, man, and woman. God made marriage and He is an integral person in a Christian marriage. If He is not actually enjoyed in your marriage, you have bought into a secular paradigm.

2. Sex is bad and dirty.

Sex was happening before the fall. All mammals were told to go forth and multiply, including mankind. Sex was and is holy in marriage. God is in support of us having a great sex life. Holding onto negative paradigms about sex can cripple any marriage.

3. Our money is ours.

No, your money is God's. He asks you to give 10% to your local church. Every single couple I've counseled who have had significant financial difficulty didn't tithe. If you think all your money is yours, you may suffer financial stress in your marriage. This "mine" mentality can be found in other areas of the marriage other than money.

4. I'm right.

If you buy into the paradigm that you're right, most conflicts or opportunities for growth become about you and you being right, which creates an adversary relationship with your spouse and any of their great and helpful ideas. Being right is a curse, which limits you from learning from others and cancels the much-needed journey to discover the best solution.

5. My gender entitles me to...

In Christ there is no male or female (Galatians 3:28). Using your gender for hierarchy or control is not only sad, it's dangerous. Marriage is between three people—the King of Kings, God, is the only king in your marriage. All others are servants of Him and each other. For more on this read my book *Servant Marriage*.

6. I'm here to be served.

This paradigm is fatally flawed. When you're married, you're called into a life-long service of the other person. How well we serve our spouse will be evaluated by God, not how well we demanded service. This immaturity can rot a Christian marriage from the inside out.

7. I can't be wrong.

Since we're all sinners, we all make mistakes. Humbly accepting our flaws and taking responsibility when we're wrong is part of our Christian walk toward everyone, especially our spouse. If you haven't asked for forgiveness from your spouse, you may secretly believe you didn't sin and you're not wrong.

8. Never ask for help.

As Christians we're part of the body of Christ. We're interdependent upon each other. My experience is often the wisdom I'm lacking already exists in someone else. If I'm humble enough to ask for help from another, I'm almost always helped. When someone has the level of pride that they're supposed to know all the answers they'll fall hard. This is a dangerous paradigm to live with in marriage.

These are only a few of the dangerous paradigms people have wholeheartedly believed prior to coming to my office. Their hearts believed these as true. Their behavior reflected their embracement of these paradigms. Their marriage deeply paid the price for these false beliefs.

As we progress, I want to show you a much easier way. I want to show you the way to be a lover-spouse and have an incredible lovership with your spouse all the days of your life.

How well we serve our spouse will be evaluated by God, not how well we demanded service.

What is a Lover-Spouse?

Every journey has its first step. This is also true of the man, woman or couple who want to go from where they're at in their marriage to becoming lover-spouses.

Where we are in our marriage may be a good, stable place or a volatile, fragile place. Whether you've been married for a year or multiple decades, you've experienced the ups and downs and various seasons of marriage.

Oh, and here is another variable in your journey of marriage—not only do your circumstances change but you and your spouse change along the way! You begin your marriage from that bright-eyed, bushy-tailed couple in your first apartment to the first house with children, multiple responsibilities, and changing roles and priorities. Trying to balance both of your lives as you both mature—hopefully at least.

What we graciously call maturing is you both actually changing, pure and simple. You and your spouse used to believe and act in a certain way toward each other but now that's become different—more calm shall we say.

Then there are the changes you and your spouse individually go through. There are shadows in their life that they've either faced or keep running from. They've been altered by a storm or crisis that has come into their life. You, or they, may have become less fit, more cautious, or sadly, even indifferent in areas of your lives.

Change is the one absolutes of life. We all experience change and depending on the paradigms we're operating upon; our marriage can move from a vibrant lovership during dating and the early years into a functionship.

A functionship is when romance takes a vacation from the marriage. The couple loses sight of who or why they married and focuses on the management aspect of the marriage and family.

> *A functionship is when romance takes a vacation from the marriage.*

Functionships are really common in Christian marriages especially if your theology focuses more on doing the "right thing" more than being loving. The functionship focuses on the many things that have to happen on the day-to-day basis: who's paying the bills; who's making the money; who's saving money; who's taking the children to school, picking them up, and taking them to their various activities; and who's handling all the errands including church, working out, dry cleaners, managing the fix-it guy, the yard, dishes and laundry.

When a couple moves toward functionship, there's less time just for each other. The couple often stops praying together, engaging in physical touch slows way down, and sex becomes more of a "have to" than "get to" attitude. You go to bed tired and life and marriage are no longer fun for either of you.

If a functionship becomes the norm for a couple, both individuals lower their expectations of love and passion, and accept the grind as normal. Since both silently agree to just accept this functionship life-style, there seems to be an understanding that this is just the way things are and possibly the way they always will be.

However, over time the unmet emotional connection; the lack of spiritual connection, genuine praise, and appreciation; and the resignation to the attitude of just having sex and not being made love to begins to take a toll. When this happens, an individual or the couple might build up resentment or hopelessness, which causes internal pain and conflict.

When the marriage is suffering, one or both people in the marriage have to adapt to survive this lack of being in a lovership. They might over work, over eat, over exercise, watch pornography, have emotional affairs to medicate the pain of being in a function-ship. Sadly, when an individual or the couple adapt by self-medicating to survive a functionship, that self-medicating method can then actually become an addiction or a greater problem for the marriage.

Remember this is a slow process. This process is sim-ilar to the metaphor of the proverbial frog in the pot.

This behavior in the marriage of not feeling appreciated, respected, heard, and connected occurs month after month, year after year. The decision to medicate starts off very slow--extra alcohol, racier pictures, more sharing outside the marriage, going out to eat with others, and spending extra hours at work.

{ When the marriage is suffering, one or both people in the marriage have to adapt to survive this lack of being in a lovership. }

Many of the couples I work with during Intensives can see the increase of entertainment outside the marriage, and excess volunteering and church activities as out of control once they enter therapy, but rarely could they see it as the "medicine" for the functionship as it was growing and creating a rift.

This is when one or both individuals might go into counseling to stop the medicating behavior and not so much to deal with the pain from being in a functionship. This person might fail again and again because the pain from the lack of being in a lovership has not ended.

The functionship will eventually create a crisis for the marriage. How the couple navigates and takes responsibility for this can make the difference if this marriage will survive or not.

Functionship was never God's plan for marriage. He designed marriage to be a lovership of three people—Himself, Adam, and Eve. The design of a "one being trinity on earth as it is in heaven" was his last masterpiece of creation.

Functionship was never God's plan for marriage.

Now the three being one heavenly trinity is one based on amazing love and respect for each other. This was God's biggest dream that we humans, especially those of us that are saved and filled with His word and spirit, would choose to be motivated by love toward our spouse.

We all know the story: God created man, then Eve, then His final creation, marriage. We all also know what happens in Genesis 3 when the couple ate the apple and fell into sin. This caused a huge separation between God and the other two in His marriage creation.

However, Glory to God, because Christ came all of that sin has been paid for. In Christ we have gained more than sin has taken from mankind.

Now we can, as believers, participate in the full dream of God to have a triune being, loving and giving themselves to each other on a constant basis. When we understand that we get to be married to God and our spouse, marriage can truly be a lovership for all of our days.

He now truly empowers us to kill our sin nature and not always be self-focused and instead lovingly serve our spouse. We can honestly participate in the lovership of God in marriage. A lovership is when we not only believe we can be a lover to our spouse every day, we actually authentically behave this way.

Herein lies the real trick. You can't be a lover your whole life if you don't "believe" you can. You probably won't be a lover to your spouse if you don't even think that is the goal in marriage.

> *A lovership is when we not only believe we can be a lover to our spouse every day, we actually authentically behave this way.*

You see, our behavior tells us what we actually and truly believe. If you believe you are a lover for life like I do, you're more likely to move toward actually being a lover. You want to be creative and expressive toward your spouse .

If at the end of the day you asked yourself, 'Was I a great lover to my spouse? To my God?' this would invoke great insight into how you're actually behaving toward your spouse.

If you ask yourself, 'Was I a good husband/wife today?' you would probably go through your role definition and answer accordingly. So, you can always track what you actually believe about anything including marriage based on your actual behavior.

Imagine waking up in love with your spouse rather than feeling like you are in some philosophical, duty-based, check-off-the-box of being a good husband or wife state of mind. Instead you wake up wowed and feel the same way you were enamored by them when you first held hands or kissed.

You can have a lovership like this if you both remain having the attitude of a lover-spouse and avoid being just husband and wife. Being a husband and wife is the name society gives your relationship but being a lover is who you are to your spouse.

> *You can have a lovership like this if you both remain having the attitude of a lover-spouse and avoid being just husband and wife.*

I honestly have never struggled with this husband concept. I never created some box to check off which said that if I did XYZ I could stop trying because I arrived. I was committed to be Lisa's lover all the days of my life. I know the pastor said, "I now pronounce you husband and wife." Somehow those words of having a role must have truly passed me by. I felt more like, 'wow I get a lover *and* I get to be a lover till death do us part.'

I feel extremely passionate about being a lover-spouse. Being Lisa's lover-spouse allows me to truly understand my real relationship toward Lisa. I'm her cheerleader, greatest supporter, coach, encourager, friend, the person she spends her time with, her sexual partner, and I enjoy every aspect of her. I'm unashamedly her lover-spouse.

I have a whole book to share with you about being and enjoying being a lover-spouse. I first want you to be grounded in God and His word about love.

When we really break down and examine the whole creation and redemption story, you can sum it up in one word: love. I want to walk through a distinct part of scripture to show you God's priority of love. When we see how He sees and respond to His love and wisdom, we become much more like Him. Honestly, I think the entire journey of marriage has quite a bit to do with becoming like Christ.

In Matthew 22:34-40 we see Jesus in one of those familiar settings in which religious leaders are trying to trap Jesus with well thought out questions. The first question had to do with taxes. The next about marriage and the resurrection. Then after the Sadducee failed, the Pharisees thought they would ask Jesus that "gotcha" question to trap Jesus.

> *Honestly, I think the entire journey of marriage has quite a bit to do with becoming like Christ.*

You really have to love the patient part of Jesus' personality with these religious, academic thinking types. In verse 36 the Pharisees asked "Teacher, which is the greatest commandment in the law?"

This would probably have been a really hard question for the academic types. Back then they might have had to look up a bunch of scrolls and examine and weigh each law. However, this was not a tough question for Jesus. He came from Heaven, He knows the author of the law intimately. He knows the author's heart.

Imagine the Pharisees face when Jesus didn't even take a second to answer. Jesus didn't pause and say, "let me think about that one for a while." He didn't need to ask anyone else. He knew the answer cold and answered this academic's question. In verse 37 Jesus replied, "Love the Lord your God with all your heart and with all your soul and with all your mind."

This is the first and greatest commandment, and the second one is similar. It reads, "Love your neighbor as yourself. All the law and the prophets hang on these two commandments."

This conversation with the Pharisees and Jesus is one of those amazing conversations that give you a window into the heart and mind of God. Jesus knows the Father. He knows the Father's heart and that His heart is all about love. As believers we know this Biblical truth, intuitively in our spirit we know above all we are to love God and love others.

I think we can easily suggest that loving or being a lover is very important to God. I believe that placing a priority on love in general is necessary. However, I also believe this truth of being a lover to God and others also applies specifically to being a lover to your spouse.

How can we truly say we love God who we cannot see and not love our spouse who we get to see every day? When I say love I mean all-in love. I don't mean "I told you I love you years ago and I haven't changed my mind" kind of love.

> { *I think we can easily suggest that loving or being a lover is very important to God.* }

Love, by definition, is expressing. Not expressing is not loving well. As Christians we learn early on John 3:16: "God so loved the world that He gave His only begotten son." To love is to give, not to withhold giving.

Lover-spouses know this at a very intuitive level, but anyone can learn to be a lover-spouse. It's in all of us to a be lover-spouse.

We're called to be a lover-spouse, not managing partners of a family enterprise. We're not following some code or law to love our spouse. We're lovers. We're commanded to love because it's who we are and it's about being the best of who we are.

I've trained thousands of couples to become better lovers of their spouses. When they're in love with their spouse, not only can the marriage change—they change! The one thing I absolutely know, both personally and professionally, is love changes us. If I allow love to flow through me toward someone, they become a soul of value. I immediately give them the respect or honor of being God's child regardless of their beliefs or behaviors.

> { *We're called to be a lover-spouse, not managing partners of a family enterprise.* }

I've seen countless times when a man or woman reopens their heart to love their spouse. This love changes not only the person giving it but the person receiving it. Imagine if the real plan was a proactive loving of our spouse. In this process we would daily change to be more Christ-like and probably more fun to be around.

When men and women are intentionally lovers toward their spouse, they feel better about themselves. When we're responsible with the blessings God has given us, because all good gifts are from God, we feel better.

If I maintain my car, my house, and my toys of any kind, I feel responsible and respectful to God. Upholding our spouses by being their lovers is one of the greatest feelings you can have.

When you love well, you feel well. When we love our spouse as unto the Father, we're saying from our heart, "Thank you for this amazing person being in my life. I'm happy to bless, encourage, and strengthen them."

I have adult children. When they marry, my biggest hope is they're loved well. When you're loved well and loving well, life is just better because you're walking with your best friend who loves you with all their heart.

I feel great when I buy Lisa a card, plan a get-away, give her flowers or just spend quality time giving her a well-deserved foot rub. Being a lover is fun and brings out your creativity so that you feel great about being a lover-spouse.

{ When you're loved well and loving well, life is just better because you're walking with your best friend who loves you with all their heart. }

A spouse that gives the minimum tolerates instead of celebrates their spouse, doesn't feel good about themselves and quite frankly shouldn't. Failing at anything or not being responsible at anything doesn't feel good. Failing at marriage really doesn't feel good. When we stand before all our friends and family and promise to love and fulfill that promise, we feel greater. Keeping our word makes us feel a lot better than not keeping our word.

When we don't keep our word to be a lover for a life-time to our spouse, we know it. We know we're not all in, we're not trying, we gave up, and we now have to live with the fact that we are both doing and being less than we promised.

We can be honest and take responsibility for our lack of love, which would be healthy. However, such honesty would spur us to most likely change. If we're not honest then we need to blame someone or something, so we feel less guilty for our lack of love.

I have counseled many spouses who had to stop blaming life, the kids, their finances, work obligations, age, or culture for their lack of love. When we remain in blaming mode, we can't heal what is wrong in our heart or life.

In my more than thirty years of counseling, I've yet to meet a person who is a functional spouse doing the basics or minimum toward their spouse say, "I feel great about the way I treat my spouse." They don't admit that deep down they know they're not giving their marriage or their spouse their best. They know they're not truly being Godly because to be Godly would be to be a lover. They know they're not all in and being selfish, which feels terrible.

Such low marriage-esteem can then continue to grow to negatively impact the marriage. Imagine two people who know they're not all-in love with their spouse. They promised God, family, and friends they'd all-in love their spouse but are failing spectacularly on a daily basis. Both individuals feel like failures because they are. They both know they're liars because they are. They both know they're in direct disobedience to the Spirit of God within them.

This scenario creates resentment and hopelessness toward their spouse for being so irresponsible with their heart, spirit and sexuality. It's also the perfect scenario to build up guilt, shame, and lowered self-esteem. The longer they function instead of being in all-in love, the worse everyone feels.

However, and thankfully, our God is a God of mercy and true love. Regardless of any sin we commit, He's not only willing to forgive us but empowers us to overcome that sin. I can hear some of you quietly thinking, 'it's not a sin the way I treat my spouse.' For some of you it's not because you're already a lover-spouse and these pages are only going to validate that you're a lover-spouse. However, many might feel conviction of their lack of loving their spouse as a sin. James 4:17 states, "Anyone then, who knows the good he ought to do and doesn't do it, sins."

Some of us reading these pages know a lot about how to love our spouse. We know what blesses them and makes them feel special, yet others often intentionally don't do it. This is a sin.

Logically if not doing it is sin, then doing it is something really good. As believers it's a priority to all of us to hear from the Father at the end of our lives, "Well done good and faithful servant."

We know we want to hear such words said about who we are at work, by our neighbors, and church family but I believe the greatest place to hear "well done good and faithful servant" is in our marriage.

Our marriage provides a daily opportunity to serve in various capacities, including demonstrating the nature of Christ to our spouse and doing so in such a way that we're all-in lover-spouses toward the one we married.

Our Father in Heaven deserves our absolute best in being lovers to our spouse. After all, God's not just our Father, He's our Father-in-law. How we treat our spouse deeply affects the way God feels about you.

{ *Our Father in Heaven deserves our absolute best in being lovers to our spouse.* }

If you're an all-in lover-spouse toward your spouse, this makes Him happy with you. If, however, you're just functioning, tolerating or, even worse, withholding, He's not happy with you as a son- or daughter-in-law.

Take a moment and really think about God as your Father-in-law. Close your eyes and guess at what He feels about you. What would He say to you as your in-law? Would He be proud, hurt, disgusted?

I've conducted many men's and marriage conferences. Every time I share that God isn't just your Father but your Father-in-law, light bulbs go on. When I pray, "Father-in-law God" I feel the honest accountability as a lover-spouse to my wife.

God is her creator and her designer. Her God is huge. Her being a daughter of the most high elevates Lisa to where she should be in my heart because that's where she is in His heart.

Our spouse is worthy of us being an all-in lover. This isn't based on their performance towards us. They're worthy because our Savior Christ Jesus made them worthy through His death and resurrection. They're worth His blood because He says so. So, they're worthy of us being awesome lover-spouses.

Lastly, you're worthy of feeling you did your best and loved your best. You're worth the awareness that you were an all-in lover toward your spouse!

When I pray,
"Father-in-law God" I feel
the honest accountability as
a lover-spouse to my wife.

The Promises

"In the beginning" are probably my favorite three words to start a thought. It's these three words that start the entire unfolding of all the scriptures.

These words are important because before God created time, so He could then create a world in which His children lived, time didn't exist. After the drama of mankind's story is fulfilled, time will be gone, and we'll live eternally with the Father.

In time however, there are continuous beginnings. There was the creation of the earth; the atmosphere; and the formation of creatures including man and woman; and then the masterpiece of the first marriage between God, man, and woman.

Since the dawn of time, God has created billions of marriages. It's quite likely that He will create billions of more marriages before time breathes her last breath.

However, in all those billions and billions of marriages there was the unique and memorable beginning of your marriage. In western culture the bride and groom invest so much time in planning the wedding, which includes her celebration before the wedding, his celebration with his friends, and finally, there is the BIG day.

The groom was so handsome in his tuxedo or suit. The bride was wearing, probably, the most expensive dress of her life. The groomsmen stood at the altar. The bride chose her favorite song with which to make her grand entrance. We all stand, and the ceremony begins.

As an associate pastor I've officiated some weddings and I've also been to several as a guest. In every wedding there's some version of what I call the four promises that the preacher asks each of the couples before they're proclaimed as man and wife.

Let's walk through these four promises almost every couple knowingly made to each other before God, family, and friends. I want to review what we promised each other because I believe with all my heart we promised to be lovers for the rest of our lives. I believe we make a covenant to be lover spouses from this day until death. But somehow walking away with the title "husband and wife" overshadowed our promises to be lovers for a lifetime.

Promise #1

I'm sure you remember as I do as clear as if it was yesterday the feeling of standing in front of the crowd of family and friends with the pastor before us. He asked the first promise to each of us individually in the form of a question.

"Do you promise to forsake all others?" We generally acknowledged in some way "I do." This is the first promise we committed to being a lover-spouse. In its most simple meaning to a young twenty-year-old couple, they interpret that promise as being "you will not have any other girlfriend or boyfriends other than this person standing in front of you the rest of your life." However, this promise goes way deeper and continues to grow in meaning over time.

The promise to forsake all others means much more than not having other romantic or sexual relationships, but let's first explore this primary aspect of the promise we've made.

> The promise to forsake all others means much more than not having other romantic or sexual relationships.

We all know a Christian couple who have been damaged and divorced because of some form of infidelity. Circumstances surrounding the dissolution of their marriage might involve a long sexual affair, a one-night stand, an anonymous encounter from someone via the Internet or even paid-for sex.

I counsel couples struggling with infidelity. Couples fly in to Colorado Springs on a weekly basis to visit my offices from all over the world to attend Intensive sessions to repair all forms of infidelity.

When a couple models their marriage after the paradigm of husband and wife, they create a set of rules to perform by. They can tend to move toward more of a functionship than a relationship and stop really being lovers.

Quietly they begin to feel less a priority to their spouse because in a functionship, the priority is managing the marriage around all the other priorities. The task of managing those other priorities has replaced connection, quality time, and dreaming together. Dating has lost its priority and sex has moved to familiar or "have-to" attitude rather than a "get to" attitude.

Pain begins to impact the marriage. This pain was either created within the marriage due to infidelity or another betrayal or is due to issues one or both the individuals didn't deal with prior to the marriage.

Let's quickly touch upon the matter about repairing past issues. Such issues can consist of family of origin stuff, prior romantic/sexual relationships, abortion, alcohol, drug or pornography addictions. These issues can contribute to how honest or mature you can be in your marriage. I will address this further in a future chapter. However, the following biblical illustration expresses how important God thought it was to heal before marriage.

Genesis 2:20-21: "But for Adam no suitable helper was found. So, the Lord God caused the man to fall into a deep sleep; and while he was sleeping, he took one of the man's ribs and closed up the place with flesh."

After God anesthetized Adam, performed surgery, he "closed up" Adam or healed him. God did not want Adam's marriage, or any marriage for that matter, to be based on one person's pain. Our pain, regardless of what it was from our past, is ours to allow God to heal. If you didn't work on your past pain before marriage, then attack these issues as soon as possible.

> { *Our pain, regardless of what it was from our past, is ours to allow God to heal.* }

Let's return to the couple who have drifted into a dry functional marriage, or a functionship as we call it. This couple needs to treat the pain in some way. Some turn to God and pray while others turn to helpful resources, books, counseling, and marriage seminars. Sadly, however, some turn to "others" and "others" can be a plethora of options. Turning to others begins to erode the promise we made to one another to forsake all others.

Let's explore what those "other" options that I've seen begin to erode or actually break that early promise to forsake all others. The obvious choice is the one everyone thinks of first: adultery. The husband or wife engages in a sex act—hand, oral or vaginal--either one time or ongoing. This act could include one or many people.

A long-term affair can take place with one person over years or decades. Multiple affairs can include prostitutes, strip clubs, lap dances, and adult book stores including any gender.

I can attest to the fact that I've met many "religious" people who believe that as long as they didn't actually have a sex act with an actual other person that they were keeping their wedding vow promise to their spouse. This promise can be utilized very legalistically within the Christian community.

When one commits to or feels strongly about the deeper spirit of the promise to forsake "all others" that isn't just defined as having sex outside of marriage, then the promise is a priority promise. This means that I put you above all other people or circumstances. As Christians, God always comes first. Second should be our spouse. Lovers know this intuitively. However, the paradigm of some husbands and wives might exclude this priority after marriage.

Genesis 2:24: "For this reason, a man will leave his father and mother and be united to his wife. And they will become one flesh." Even in the first marriage where there were no parents, God made clear what the priorities of marriage are.

Just recently, I counseled a couple who shortly after marriage, made the decision that the man would work for his father. They both communicated to me in counseling that his heart was more focused on pleasing his father than his wife and this behavior went on for many years. In my more than thirty years of counseling, I've heard wives complain about their husband's loyalty to a father, mother or siblings over them. I've also heard from husbands who've felt their wife was more committed to her parents or family than to him.

To be faithful and forsake all others includes prioritizing your family of origin, including your parents, over your spouse. Of course, you should have a loving relationship with these people but make sure to evaluate the priority of these relationships and how these priorities affect your marriage. It needs to be said that forsaking all these others is not just a problem among women. Both spouses struggle here regularly.

Forsaking all others also means you prioritize your own children in such a way that your marriage remains the priority. I am in full support of women who want to be great mothers, but I've repeatedly seen this as an excuse not to be great lovers to their spouse. In these situations, dating the spouse ceases, the woman rarely expresses affection and praise, she lacks the energy or urgency to prioritize sex, she has no time for dates or fun or weekend away here and there. These are all symptoms of a woman who has moved from a lover-spouse to prioritizing her children or her role to be a "good mom" over her husband.

Men can also over prioritize their children over their wife, although this is more common in later years or after he retires. The wife feels he's always helping the children with projects, time, or money. He stops prioritizing her, becomes too tired for her, ceases sex and stops expressing affection as well.

> { *Forsaking all others also means you prioritize your own children in such a way that your marriage remains the priority.* }

Forsaking all others includes <u>all others</u>. You can also evaluate whether friends hold too high a value in either of your lives. I've had to work with men who give way too much time to a set of guy friends or friend by scheduling hunting and fishing trips or golf outings. He had to adjust priorities. It didn't mean he had to stop his activities. He just had to adjust his activities. I've had to deal with a "golf widow." That's what a wife is called when her husband golfs all weekend, most weekends. Her husband adjusted to one time per week and that felt fine to everyone.

Women can also overprioritize friendships and/or social activities such as making excessive or long phone calls, Facebook perusing, attending athletic activities and volunteering. She can over involve, over value, and over invest her heart and time in these relationships. In other marriage books, I've written about the value of same-gender relationships but there must be balance.

Church family is also another set of people we must balance in our life. I'm a church-loving guy. I love going to church. Through the years Lisa and I have been involved in various forms of groups, activities, and leadership positions. However, some couples or individuals can overprioritize the church or "their ministry." For all involved, forsaking all others also means that you find balance with how you dedicate your time to your church.

Community is also another group of people we need to evaluate. Examples of community are volunteering or just participating in community events. Again, in balance this is healthy and great for a couple to enjoy or contribute in events locally or even globally. You must evaluate your priorities in the area of volunteering and community and create a balance so you can keep your promise to forsake all others.

You should now take a moment to reflect, evaluate and ask yourself whether there's a family member, friend or group of people that you overprioritize. Remember, you're a lover-spouse, so as a lover-spouse, your husband or wife should feel and believe they're the most important soul to you in the whole wide world.

Lisa and I recently went away for a weekend, just the two of us. She felt we both needed to get away from the house and work projects, including this book. As we were walking back to the hotel from a meal, my wife just randomly starts explaining how she appreciated how good of friends we are and the various pet names I've given her over the years that reflect our deep connection.

Lisa has always been my priority—during my education, through parenting, with business, and in projects. For instance, during this season in my life I have been getting up at 5:00 a.m. to write this book so we can have more time together. Because I'm her lover, I want more time with her, so I wake up early to knock out some household chores and write so I get more time with my lover today.

Promise #2

After the pastor asks you if you'll forsake all others, he continues to have you make three more promises or covenants before God, family, and friends. Usually we're so enraptured by looking at our soon-to-be spouse, we may not be carefully listening to the promises we're actually making.

I want to unpack those next three promises that often are stated in one sentence during your marriage ceremony. Do you promise to love, honor, and cherish... and then you say those forever-binding two words of "I do!"

Let's examine these three promises in slow motion and initially focus on the first one. Do you promise to love your spouse?

With this covenant, you're promising to be their lover for life. When you promise to love, you're promising to be their lover. Promising to be a lover-spouse to one person is a really big promise. For me, I was happy to be Lisa's lover for life. That's actually why I married her. I wanted to wake up with her, praise her, nurture her, touch her, eat with her, do whatever during the day, and be together all night. That sounded and still sounds like an awesome idea!

{ *When you promise to love, you're promising to be their lover.* }

When a couple moves away from the promise to be each other's lover, they tend to move away from a lovership into a functionship. This doesn't have to happen, but often it does as they define themselves by husband and wife as opposed to lovers for life.

You know exactly who you are or who you've become in your marriage toward your wife or husband. You absolutely know whether there's enough tangible evidence to convict you of being a lover toward your spouse. Hopefully there's enough evidence that anyone—family, friend, a lawyer, or God Himself could state, "Wow, the evidence is so great that you are guilty of being your spouse's lover all of these years."

For many who I've counseled with over the years in marriage intensives or met when conducting or attending marriage conferences, they couldn't be found guilty of being that lover over the years or decades to their spouse.

Sadly, the facts support that they function as a husband or wife, not as lovers. They would be guilty of being good at the functions of marriage but not at being awesome lovers toward their spouse.

What's particularly interesting is that before they married, they were really guilty of being lovers. They didn't need a marriage conference to be kind to their lover. They were intuitive, patient, and understanding. They graciously overlooked their girlfriend's or boyfriend's foibles and flaws.

They weren't easily offended and tried to understand the other person. They over-communicated about their life to each other. They made each other a priority by spending regular time together and dating each other without paying a therapist to tell them to date. They shared their heart, dreams, and feelings naturally. To be with each other was in itself a joyful event. To be absent was painful in a real heartfelt way.

Everything the other person did for them was appreciated, praised, and remembered. You heard each other's desires and preferences and it was a joy to provide that for them. Physical affections didn't need to be scripted. You didn't have to tell each other about your need for touch. You could barely keep your hands off each other. You didn't know it but you were being lovers. You had amazing value and top priority without any need for external motivation. You were lovers from the inside out. Your lover had amazing value and top priority and you didn't need a self-help book because it was in you to love them.

You were so good at loving them that they wanted to sign up for the way you love for the rest of their lives.

That's the kind of love you promised before God, friends, and family. You promised to be that kind of lover to your spouse until death do you part.

Here's the amazing thing, you already know how to be your spouse's lover because you're guilty of being their lover before marriage. This behavior toward your spouse was a reality when you were dating. These aren't sermons, books or DVDs you watched of someone else being a lover to someone you never met.

> *Here's the amazing thing, you already know how to be your spouse's lover because you're guilty of being their lover before marriage.*

In your dating you defined yourself at some point as their lover, and when you did, loving them was easy and natural. That's why it was so easy to commit to continue to be their lover because it was easy to love them.

 Promise #3

You agreed to honor your spouse. The way I like to frame honoring your spouse is to put them in a high place in your heart.

What I mean by this is you not only consider them, but you prioritize them. My wife Lisa is absolutely amazing at honoring me. She will think through a problem whether it is business, personal, or regarding our children. She'll have mulled this issue for hours, days or even weeks and consider various options. Even on small issues, she'll weigh her ideas and then present her ideas to me for a solution.

I've always felt honored by Lisa. She holds me high in her heart and considers and values me. Some might call this honoring or respect.

When you were dating your spouse, you were probably quite guilty of honoring them maybe even over-honoring them. In your twenties, when your then girlfriend or boyfriend had a different idea or approach to an idea than your parents you might've gone with the girlfriend's or boyfriend's idea even over the wisdom of your parents.

Back then your spouse didn't need to demand honor or respect from you. They didn't need to quote scripture to get honor from you. You freely gave honor to them because you highly valued them as a person, a soul.

You wanted to hear their thoughts, heart or opinion about issues you were experiencing. You leaned into their experience and ideas for solving problems. You respected their ideas even when you disagreed. You thought more as a practical team than just "me." There was an "us" consciousness about decisions you made and how that could impact the other person.

You were probably not only guilty of over-communicating your world to them, you were also guilty of over-listening about their feelings and concerns.

You didn't roll your eyes, act impatient, finish their sentence, put down their ideas, call them stupid or act like a two-year-old when your ideas were challenged. You didn't withhold love when you didn't get your way. If you acted this disrespectfully toward them and they still married you even though you already had a pattern of dishonoring them and overvaluing yourself then they knew full well they were entering a lifetime of disrespect and dishonor.

However, if you changed from an honoring, considerate person to become a person who disrespects and under values the soul and heart of your spouse then you're not keeping the promise of honoring your spouse.

You might need to look at the path you took to become less respectful and honoring of your spouse. Don't use this opportunity to look to their sin to blame them for why you changed. You clearly knew you were marrying a sinner. That was your only choice since no one is perfect.

Who you became in the story of your marriage is 100 percent your responsibility. I've seen men and women address huge amounts of sin and betrayal, authority being stole from them, public humiliation, and still remain respectful of the other person.

I've also seen self-absorbed children in marriage who are so disrespectful and dishonoring of their spouse I have to correct them like a parent in my office. I have to ask them to respect their spouse or leave my office.

Honor is a heart issue. When you honor you say, "My heart respects the value of your heart." When you disrespect the heart of your spouse, you'll often act in many immature ways that makes it a challenge to honor you.

I'm always amazed at Bible-believing Christians who have heard hundreds of times about sowing and reaping then think they can sow seeds of disrespect in their marriage and think this will bring fruit of honor. So, if you've moved from a place of honoring your spouse to a place of dishonoring them, you'll treat them more like an object of distain than a soul of unmeasurable value. If this occurs, the very fuel for being a lover would leave you.

> When you disrespect the heart of your spouse, you'll often act in many immature ways that makes it a challenge to honor you.

Marriage will become a "have to" instead of a "get to" to you. Keeping your promise to honor your spouse for a lifetime is fundamental if you're to be a lover-spouse.

Hear me as I say from my heart that honoring anyone for decades is a heart commitment. Such a commitment requires lots of hard work. To honor is to sometimes look past some emotional and spiritual immaturity of the moment and see the bigger picture of who this person really is.

Promise #4

Do you promise to love, honor, and cherish this man or woman until death do you part? Cherishing is the final promise you declared before God, family, and friends.

Cherish is a unique word. To me, cherish means to make the other person feel special. You not only are the primary person in your spouse's life who knows their strengths and weaknesses, but you also know what makes them feel special or cherished. You knew how to make them feel special or cherished during dating. You knew the special days or events that hold meaning to your then girlfriend or boyfriend.

You knew the special places they liked to go and you'd invite them to these places. You knew the activities that meant something to your then boyfriend or girlfriend—a bike ride, a ride in the truck, a sporting event or some form of entertainment. You knew their favorite ice cream, pie, meal, pizza toppings and clothes. You knew what and who they valued and you made them feel important and cherished.

Cherishing your spouse tells them "I love you, I want you to know I see you, and want you to know you're very special to me." I love cherishing Lisa in everything from foot massages, long talks, or the sticky notes to remember that the St. Patrick's Day parade is an annual event for us.

Cherishing is something you promised to do. Look over the last week, month, year or decade(s). Verify if there's a trail of cherishing your spouse. I mean more than the culturally-obligatory days like birthdays, anniversaries, and Christmas. I mean random acts of "I think you're awesome."

Do you still write notes of kindness or love? Do you text loving statements? Are you proactively articulating something or some event to make them feel special?

If so great! If not, why?

You promised to be a lover for life. A lover-spouse never stops making the other person feel special whether that is via a back rub, a sexual behavior, special gift or creating a special event you know they would enjoy.

If your cherishing creative ideas have dried up from how it was during your dating days, your spouse might legitimately feel like a bait and switch has occurred. They might feel "You promised to cherish me but I have so little proof of this." I hope that's not your story.

{ *A lover-spouse never stops making the other person feel special...* }

I hope your spouse can think of something recently on how you cherished them. Cherishing is where you build memories and a narrative to your spouse that "I still see you, I still think you're awesome and amazing and here's the proof in this gift, activity, or event that I planned for you."

I understand the challenges of life pre-children, raising children, and as empty nesters. However, lovers never make excuses. Lovers make plans. As a lover-spouse you might need to make a list of what makes your spouse feel special. Then put these in your cell phone and follow through.

Cherishing is not an intention. Cherishing is a behavior you thought about doing then you followed through and now it's a love memory your spouse has which validates that you cherish them. Cherishing presents things I'm planning. You're a lover-spouse so cherishing becomes a lifestyle.

Lovers make plans. As a lover-spouse you might need to make a list of what makes your spouse feel special.

Love without Lover

Mary and John have flown in from the Northeast to attend a marriage Intensive. It's Monday and they begin to share that the reason they're here is because although they love each other they're not in love any more.

Mary and John are not uncommon. They got married in their early twenties and have raised four boys that have left home.

They've had a friendship for decades. They paid bills, ran errands, fixed up homes, both worked in their careers, and now don't look forward to coming home. Sex is rare and they're challenged to be civil. They have a general disrespect for each other but they "love" one another.

This would be a typical situation in any pastor's or

counselor's office. Mary and John are similar to so many other couples who struggle with being lovers.

As Christians we're supposed to be experts in love, and yet most of my clients that struggle with love in their marriage are Bible-believing Christians.

How can we serve a God who defines Himself as love, "God is Love" and have so many loveless marriages? I want to spend some time sharing possible reasons for this contrast.

Let's start off with a bit of a theological discussion to see if one can get some solutions. As we mentioned, God is love. He would still be God and would be right and just even if every human spent an eternity in hell. However, this is not what love does. When love exists, it exists in the form of a verb not a noun form. Love not only moves toward the other, love opens up the flood gates and gives all. In short, love shows up and shows up in a big way.

{ *When love exists, it exists in the form of a verb not a noun form.* }

We see this amazing love of God throughout the Old Testament. God's love supernaturally gave Abraham a son. God provided the sacrifice when Abraham was willing to sacrifice Isaac. God loved Israel and provided for her lovingly through Joseph's leadership. God loved Israel and delivered her from Egypt. He divided the Red Sea and fed and guided them for decades. He repeatedly sent prophets and leaders to guide Israel and called her back to Himself.

You see God loved and was a lover-spouse to Israel. He regularly blessed, provided for her abundantly, and guided her. When you read through the Old Testament, you witness God as a lover. You read the stories with a romantic tone that touches your heart as you witness this massive strong God be so in love with His people He regularly breaks the rules of gravity, physical, or natural to illustrate His great love for Israel.

You see this massive God chasing Israel through the stories of the prophets. When Israel comes back to her lover God and allows Him the proper place in their lives she is blessed, safe, and prosperous. When she rejects the lover God and replaces Him with other gods, her life doesn't go so well.

We see the lover God in the Old Testament. We can see the lover God in John 3:16 which states, "For God so loved the world that he gave his one and only Son, that whoever believes in him shall not perish but have eternal life." Now let's look at the lover God in Christ Jesus.

First, He conforms himself to our human form to place Himself in a human baby's body. If He didn't do anything else, this is already a tremendous act of love. Imagine loving chihuahua's and giving up all your freedom and blessings so you could become a chihuahua puppy to live as a chihuahua so you could redeem the chihuahuas.

He lived a sinless life so He could be our sacrifice for our sins. He died a humble death by any standards so we could have eternal life. He rose from the dead and promised to give us the Holy Spirit and promises to return to rule and reign forever.

The Gospel is an amazing hero epic story based on love. Christ loved, which moved Him to leave His comforts and privileges to pursue us. He conformed himself to our human form. He honored us by living a pure life. He sacrificed himself so we could have eternal life. He promised to never leave or forsake us in our story together with Him.

This not just a hero epic story of every Christian's existence but also serves as an example for every marriage to mirror. You left the world of singleness (i.e., do what you want, freedom 24/7) to become married. You loved, you moved toward. You conformed your life around the person and circumstances of that person. You sacrificed yourself in this process of becoming one. You honor your spouse by how you protect them. You promised never to leave them in marriage. You both are part of a huge hero epic story holding the hand of each other and your Father.

I want to walk through some of those very basic points of Christ's love as they apply to being an amazing lover-spouse to your husband or wife.

First, you must leave your comfort zone in order to love. Let's explore that a little deeper. Let me brag on Lisa, my wife, for a moment. Lisa comes from a very typical, mostly German, Pennsylvania family. This particular larger tribe of people are settlers by nature. They live in the same area all their lives and rarely travel very far and even more rarely leave the state or county.

The German tribe love the sameness, steadiness of life. They love traveling the same roads, having the same friends, and even having the same job all their lives. There is pride in being dependable and faithful to whoever and whatever they commit themselves to. My Lisa is very much a part of this tribe and until this day most of her family live in the same area they grew up in.

Then my bright, green eyed Lisa fell in love with me—a poor, Bible school student who just loved Jesus. Through the years of our dating I graduated Bible school, which was in the town Lisa grew up. After Bible school, I felt called to seminary, which was in Texas. I went to Texas and felt the pain of not having Lisa in my daily life, so I asked her to marry me, which she did. We married in Pennsylvania and then went to Texas where we lived for years.

The lover in Lisa allowed her to leave all that was familiar, safe, and secure for her to be with her love, me. Leaving Pennsylvania was a big deal but loving me was a bigger deal.

In marriage there is a lot of 'leaving" your comfort zone for the other. As a lover, you want to explore their world. Their world is different than yours just like Texas is different than Pennsylvania. You want to explore them, however in this exploring you will find differences that can and will stretch you.

Your leaving your comfort zone for your spouse is an ongoing act of love. I encourage people to enjoy the ride because the destination is unknown. So often at marriage conferences or when I'm doing marriage Intensives with a couple, I hear one of them say "It's not my personality." This is their measurement—themselves. I explain how marriage is dying to yourself to become one, but some people really love their personality more than they love Jesus or their spouse.

{ *Your leaving your comfort zone for your spouse is an ongoing act of love.* }

This person faces real challenges in being a lover-spouse. They choose to stay within the confines of what is comfortable or suits their own personality. To be a lover-spouse you're going to have to leave you and your personality to be a great lover-spouse. You'll have to sacrifice some of yourself to create and invest into this thing called marriage.

I liken this to the creation of a child. The sperm and egg are wildly attracted to each other. They both die to themselves and the beginning of a new life starts. If the sperm or the egg says, "I love you but I'm not going to leave me to join you" there is no child. Both sacrifice all they knew to become something totally different.

As a lover-spouse you'll conform some to love your spouse. The way you think, feel and serve will be to be the best lover to your spouse. This can be the hard part as you serve mostly from a place you might be weak, such as patience, to be a lover to your spouse.

Fortunately for us as believers we do have the Holy Spirit in us, so we have unlimited access to His nature to flow through us to love our spouse. This conforming or dying to ourselves is a lifelong process. The seasons of life change who our spouse is and they mature (hopefully) and their desires become different over the decades of the marriage so this adapting to be a lover is a lifelong process.

This is actually the fun part of the journey: adaptation as your spouse grows and changes. What a husband or wife might really be blessed by in their twenties will be totally different than that same behavior in their sixties.

Here's what I've found personally and professionally is that the quicker you die to something to serve the other person, the better. If you revisit this dying to yourself through service, your disobedience to die can continue to foster pain or challenges in the marriage. Personally, as the Holy Spirit prompts you to grow and serve that is the best time to do it. I've found He is persistent, so it is best to practice dying to yourself since that's the process we're all in if we're brave enough to be married.

Honoring the one we love is an important ingredient so we can have a sacrificial life. Again, honor is valuing them. This is more than sexual purity—it's being who we need to be for our spouse.

As a psychologist, I need to have a pretty good self-care regimen and balance of life. Like a surgeon, couples come visit my offices every week to go into "operating" on their marriage, souls, and systems of believing.

> { *Honoring the one we love is an important ingredient so we can have a sacrificial life.* }

I truly honor my clients, so I maintain a fit lifestyle of regular workouts, aerobics, stretching, and eating healthy. I do this so I can be optimal for them. I pray throughout the day. I read and listen daily to the word of God. I have good relationships and a great marriage. All of this is a form of honoring my clients so I can serve with excellence.

A client just recently told me that they went to see a therapist who was immensely overweight, depressed, and had other addictions. They didn't feel this person's life was in order enough to be counseling them. They didn't feel honored by this person.

Marriage is a tough sport so having a reasonably good self-care routine helps you to serve as a lover-spouse with excellence. You feel better and age slower as a side effect.

> { *Marriage is a tough sport so having a reasonably good self-care routine helps you to serve as a lover-spouse with excellence.* }

Ongoing sacrifice is the life blood of a healthy marriage. This must be mutual sacrificing. If only one person is sacrificing, the other could still be married to themselves not their spouse. Selfishness in all its various manifestations is truly the plague on any marriage.

If selfishness exists and the nature of one or both the spouses is to love themselves first, the marriage consistently suffers. This suffering could manifest as unconfessed sins, secrets, and the hardening of hearts. The selfish individual will constantly be evaluating how well they're being served rather than evaluating how well they're serving.

When both people are honestly serving with excellence, the sacrificing work is consistent. However, as in other areas of your life, the areas you practice the most in, are the areas you become better at. Sacrificing may not always be fun but the joy of a healthy lover-spouse marriage is way more fun than a self-centered life inside of a "marriage."

The resurrection always follows death. Our sacrifices add up and over time, if both individuals are sacrificing, both become more like Christ. I can't imagine a happier ending to a story in which all of us become more like Jesus.

Now let's look at some of the ideas and teaching Jesus gave us. I think here we'll get another glimpse into this idea that love moves, and that love is not just an emotion I feel but rather a behavior of how I move toward others.

If selfishness exists and the nature of one or both the spouses is to love themselves first, the marriage consistently suffers.

Jesus Teaches On Love

Now I want to explore some very familiar territory. I have a little trepidation at the thought of doing this because revisiting familiar scripture can be like that drive home you do every day. You know when you go on autopilot and think about other things, assume you know what's going to happen therefore you don't concentrate?

I live in Colorado, and even here among some of the most beautiful terrain in the entire country you can tune out and stop that little child voice that would normally go, "Wow, amazing!"

Fortunately, I live in constant awe of my environment. I see amazing rocks, trees and forests every day and I still go "wow." Because I'm also paying attention this often helps me from hitting the foxes, squirrels, raccoon, turkeys, and larger critters that tend to think the road is a valid place to travel.

Just this morning on the way into town I saw two dead raccoons. This happens when drivers are less aware. This can also happen in marriage when we stop the "wow" when we look at our spouse, but I digress.

So, as I present the scripture, concentrate and read every word. You might actually be shown more that I'm going to comment on. The first scripture I want to explore is Matthew 25:31-46.

The Sheep and the Goats

31 "When the Son of Man comes in his glory, and all the angels with him, he will sit on his glorious throne. 32 All the nations will be gathered before him, and he will separate the people one from another as a shepherd separates the sheep from the goats. 33 He will put the sheep on his right and the goats on his left.

34 "Then the King will say to those on his right, 'Come, you who are blessed by my Father; take your inher-

itance, the kingdom prepared for you since the creation of the world. [35] For I was hungry and you gave me something to eat, I was thirsty and you gave me something to drink, I was a stranger and you invited me in, [36] I needed clothes and you clothed me, I was sick and you looked after me, I was in prison and you came to visit me.'

[37] "Then the righteous will answer him, 'Lord, when did we see you hungry and feed you, or thirsty and give you something to drink? [38] When did we see you a stranger and invite you in, or needing clothes and clothe you? [39] When did we see you sick or in prison and go to visit you?'

[40] "The King will reply, 'Truly I tell you, whatever you did for one of the least of these brothers and sisters of mine, you did for me.'

[41] "Then he will say to those on his left, 'Depart from me, you who are cursed, into the eternal fire prepared for the devil and his angels. [42] For I was hungry and you gave me nothing to eat, I was thirsty and you gave me nothing to drink, [43] I was a stranger and you did not invite me in, I needed clothes and you did not

clothe me, I was sick and in prison and you did not look after me.'

44 "They also will answer, 'Lord, when did we see you hungry or thirsty or a stranger or needing clothes or sick or in prison, and did not help you?'

45 "He will reply, 'Truly I tell you, whatever you did not do for one of the least of these, you did not do for me.'

46 "Then they will go away to eternal punishment, but the righteous to eternal life."

We could do chapters of commentary here but that's not the purpose of this book or chapter. My heart is to show you how Jesus thought about love so you and I can be awesome lover-spouses to our awesome spouse. This story is easy to dissect because Jesus gives us a few ideas to evaluate how or if we love. The lovers (sheep) value others. They value the souls of people and see all people worthy of respect and love and act as if the other has value. Do we value our spouse by how we behave toward them and their ongoing lifelong needs?

This is really a question more important to answer than just read. If you look over the last few weeks or months, how would you evaluate your love toward your spouse by behavior?

{ *My heart is to show you how Jesus thought about love so you and I can be awesome lover-spouses to our awesome spouse.* }

Imagine (those of you my age) the old Dragnet television show when the actor would say, "Just the facts, ma'am." Those younger than me might have to Google this show to understand. However, if you're looking at just behavior what would the facts conclude about how much your behavior reflects your love toward your spouse?

Love has action. The lover moves toward how they feed, clothe and visit. The lover-spouse feeds their spouse "the fruit of the spirit of love, joy, peace, forbearance, kindness, goodness, faithfulness, gentleness, self-control" (Galatians 5:22-23). When we love, we move toward our spouse.

The lover-spouse clothes their spouse. I take this to mean that you see the flaws of your spouse. When you cover them instead of exposing them to others, you cover them.

{ *When we love, we move toward our spouse.* }

The lover-spouse "visits". Visiting is often inconvenient and takes time and often some intentionality. When we're "visiting" we're making time for our spouse and giving priority to our relationship. This could be anything from daily conversational rituals such as the three dailies (i.e., pray, expressing two feelings, providing two praises), and engaging in regular date nights, overnights, and vacations with just the two of you.

What's interesting to me is how the sheep (lover-spouse) loves almost unconsciously or reflexively. The sheep had no idea what the master was talking about. They just thought it was natural to demonstrate love. For this they were blessed by the master.

Sheep/Lover-Spouse Characteristics

- Values others
- Action toward others
- Feed
- Clothe
- Visit
- Sacrifice
- Unconditionally loves

Let's turn our car up the road and visit the goat lane to contrast what love is not. This might describe the spouse who at best is a functional husband or wife or at worst a dysfunctional spouse who believes love is a noun not a verb.

Goats don't value the souls of others. They're mostly selfish, self-conscious or self-absorbed. Being goat-like would show up in the way you speak toward and behave toward your spouse. If you regularly yell, curse or put your spouse down you might not value them (goat).

Goats don't move toward their spouse's needs. When you're married to a goat you usually have to take care of your own needs. They say they love you but the amount of time that they actually move toward your need (without convincing them they should) would be infrequent.

The amount of frequency of sacrifice your spouse makes would also be infrequent and when they do engage in sacrifice, they generally want you to offer praise for it. Sacrifice, if when made is meant to be repaid, remembered, or over-valued is a goat-spouse view of life.

Unconscious unloving is amazing to me. The spouse who engages in this behavior is literally oblivious to the needs, desires, goals or dreams of their spouse. They're genuinely clueless. They're not acting clueless. They actually are clueless about why their self-absorbed, self-focused life closes their heart to the value and needs of others, including their spouse. For these attitudes the goats were cursed by the master in this parable.

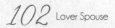

Characteristics of a goat/functional or dysfunctional spouse

- People and souls don't have value
- Inaction toward spouse
- Limited sacrifice
- Unconscious unloving

I want to spend more time here, but I think in a moment of reflection you know whether you're a sheep (lover-spouse) or a goat (functional or dysfunctional) spouse based upon this beautiful teaching of Jesus, who embodied love.

Let's get off this road and take a detour to another familiar story of Jesus contrasting love vs. non-love. Remember to stay focused as this again is familiar terrain. However, this terrain is not familiar as far as applying it to being a lover-spouse. Here is the story of the good Samaritan (Luke 10:25-37):

The Parable of the Good Samaritan

²⁵ On one occasion an expert in the law stood up to test Jesus. "Teacher," he asked, "what must I do to inherit eternal life?"

²⁶ "What is written in the Law?" he replied. "How do you read it?"

²⁷ He answered, "'Love the Lord your God with all your heart and with all your soul and with all your strength and with all your mind'; and, 'Love your neighbor as yourself.'"

²⁸ "You have answered correctly," Jesus replied. "Do this and you will live."

²⁹ But he wanted to justify himself, so he asked Jesus, "And who is my neighbor?"

³⁰ In reply Jesus said: "A man was going down from Jerusalem to Jericho, when he was attacked by robbers. They stripped him of his clothes, beat him and went away, leaving him half dead. ³¹ A priest happened to be going down the same road, and when he saw the man, he passed by on the other side. ³² So too, a Lev-

ite, when he came to the place and saw him, passed by on the other side.[33] But a Samaritan, as he traveled, came where the man was; and when he saw him, he took pity on him. [34] He went to him and bandaged his wounds, pouring on oil and wine. Then he put the man on his own donkey, brought him to an inn and took care of him. [35] The next day he took out two denarii and gave them to the innkeeper. 'Look after him,' he said, 'and when I return, I will reimburse you for any extra expense you may have.'

[36] "Which of these three do you think was a neighbor to the man who fell into the hands of robbers?"

[37] The expert in the law replied, "The one who had mercy on him."

Jesus told him, "Go and do likewise."

Here Jesus answers the expert in the law that loving God and loving others was the answer to inherit eternal life. So, clearly this story is about love and defining love for this "expert."

This story is very important to understand the religious (self-focused) people avoided the man and his needs all together. They didn't value the soul, didn't move toward the need, and didn't feed, clothe, visit, sacrifice or love unconsciously like the sheep in the other story. Rather, like a goat, they didn't value, didn't move toward, didn't feed, didn't clothe, didn't visit, didn't sacrifice, and consistently (or in this case, consciously) unloved the man who was beaten.

The good Samaritan (sheep, lover-spouse) valued the person, moved toward, fed, clothed, visited, sacrificed, loved unconsciously (reflexively), and invested his money into the care of the man in need.

These stories have so many parallels that you can't miss Jesus teaching about love. He is very clear and provides a measurable scenario to compare our heart as to whether we're lovers or not lovers toward others. I think this teaching provides a lot for us to think about as far as being a lover-spouse.

Briefly, in John 14:15 Jesus says, "if you love me, keep my commands." Love can be evaluated by looking at our behavior. I always tell my clients to believe their behavior. Behavior always tells the truth.

As a lover-spouse we can evaluate our verb "love" by how we behave toward the love of our life, our spouse. This simple assessment always gives me an honest evaluation of how I'm loving Lisa.

> As a lover-spouse we can evaluate our verb "love" by how we behave toward the love of our life, our spouse.

Last, Jesus gave us a final commandment in John 13:34, "A new command I give you: Love one another, as I have loved you, so you must love one another." I was really tempted to underline that word "must" because it jumps out at me every time I read it. That I must love is huge for me, especially as it relates to loving Lisa.

This new command comes right after Jesus washes the feet of the disciples. He had then agreed he was the teacher and he can serve with excellence then they could do the same. He then tells the disciples in verse 16, "very truly I tell you, no servant is greater than his master, nor messenger greater than the one who sent him. Now that you know these things, you will be blessed if you do them."

Jesus shows an act of serving, which was well below his social status. He did this as an illustration in essence to say, "Here is love, to value each other, move toward, to meet the needs of the other, sacrifice, and do so with all humility like you see me do."

I can think of no clearer way to illustrate what Jesus lived and taught about love than this story. As a lover-spouse we get the privilege to value, move toward, sacrifice and invest in our spouse over a lifetime and to do so with a spirit of humility almost as if unconsciously loving is our privilege.

You and I have this amazing privilege and opportunity to serve with excellence (love) our spouse daily. This calling to love them practically is a blessing. How you respond to this opportunity can expose the pride or humility of heart you're currently manifesting.

{ *You and I have this amazing privilege and opportunity to serve with excellence (love) our spouse daily.* }

Jesus was God incarnate, washing the feet of the men He created. Regardless of your number of degrees, successes, income or importance to a group of people, you and I will never be more valuable than Christ Himself. If you're "too good, smart or beautiful" to serve and love then this misjudgment of yourself and the pride and arrogance that goes with it will definitely hurt your marriage.

Marriage is a place to proactively love and serve in humility. If we're not practicing in this, we're missing the whole teaching of Jesus on love. Here again you want to look at your behavior, not what you might wish or believe you're doing but what you're actually doing with excellence with your spouse. This will help you to see if you're more on the lover-spouse side of that continuum.

Here again it doesn't matter where you are at the moment other than for honesty sake. Be very honest with yourself. It isn't too late for you to move toward being an awesome lover-spouse.

Marriage is a place to proactively love and serve in humility. If we're not practicing in this we're missing the whole teaching of Jesus on love.

You Already Know

It's Thursday morning and I've been meeting with a couple to help them go from good to a great marriage. This couple had no infidelity, porn addiction or Intimacy Anorexia. This was a ministry leader couple who had sent several really damaged marriages to us and witnessed those marriages change. However, their own marriage was lacking that "loving feeling."

They came for not just a tune-up but a rev-up of their marriage. Monday through Wednesday they worked hard on some individual issues clogging the marriage. However, we needed to move from cleaning up to really casting a vision for this awesome marriage they wanted to co-create.

Before I start my day, I pray for my clients by name. I felt led to have them perform an exercise that I have utilized on and off for a while. I'll do this on occasion to gauge whether an exercise gets consistent results. I know this one was consistent, so I asked them to try this exercise in my office.

You'll want you to pay close attention because I'm going to give you the same opportunity to do this exercise to help you become a great lover-spouse.

You, like this couple might already have a good marriage. You don't fight much, you date occasionally, you manage money well, you're satisfied with your teamwork with any children or chores, and sex is at an acceptable pace. However, the passion, playtimes, and creative loving is rare or erratic in your marriage. This exercise can help you both become lover-spouses. Marriage becomes really fun when you're both trying to be lover-spouses. When both people in the marriage are really trying it's like two cells sending energy back and forth to each other. In this loving reciprocity, marriage can consistently feel amazing to both of you.

Imagine waking up and saying, "Wow, I love being here." Imagine getting that playful text and sending one back. Imagine greeting each other at the end of the work day like a lover kissed by their lover. Imagine going to bed feeling incredible just because they're lying next to you. That's what every marriage can feel like if both are trying to be lover-spouses to each other.

{ *When both people in the marriage are really trying it's like two cells sending energy back and forth to each other.* }

Back to the ministry leader couple. I asked them to take out their notepad. At the top of the page write, "If I were your lover I would..." Then I told them without talking to each other write out in bullet point fashion the rest of that sentence.

In the following pages, I want you to do the same. I don't want you to read on beyond and skip this exercise. I want you to grab a pen or pencil or use your phone and finish this statement:

If I was your lover, I would...(for him)

1. _____
2. _____
3. _____
4. _____
5. _____
6. _____
7. _____
8. _____
9. _____
10. _____
11. _____
12. _____
13. _____
14. _____
15. _____
16. _____
17. _____
18. _____
19. _____
20. _____

If I was your lover, I would...(for her)

1. _____
2. _____
3. _____
4. _____
5. _____
6. _____
7. _____
8. _____
9. _____
10. _____
11. _____
12. _____
13. _____
14. _____
15. _____
16. _____
17. _____
18. _____
19. _____
20. _____

Now if you're reading without finishing the assignment, you might be missing an opportunity to become a better lover-spouse. Please do your assignment in writing (not in your head and give yourself credit—actually attempt to write it out and earn the credit).

So, you probably came up with a pretty good list of ways, things to do, changes in behavior, beliefs or attitudes that would allow your spouse to feel that you were intentionally being a lover-spouse.

If you both completed this exercise, your next step is to situate yourself where you can sit face to face. Read your entire list to your spouse. Don't go back and forth. Instead, just have one person go through their whole list first. Stop here and complete this before continuing.

{ *...if you're reading without finishing the assignment you might be missing an opportunity to become a better lover-spouse.* }

In the space provided, write out your responses in reading your list to each other.

♡ For Him:

What I experienced in this exercise was:

_____
_____
_____
_____
_____
_____
_____

What insights I got from my list about being a lover-spouse:

_____
_____
_____
_____
_____
_____
_____
_____

What insight did I gain from hearing my spouse read their list to me?

_____
_____
_____
_____
_____
_____
_____
_____

For Her:

What I experienced in this exercise was:

_____
_____
_____
_____
_____
_____
_____

What insights I got from my list about being a lover-spouse:

_____
_____
_____
_____
_____
_____
_____
_____

What insight did I gain from hearing my spouse read their list to me?

_____
_____
_____
_____
_____
_____
_____

What is universally amazing to me no matter what age, color, religion or country a couple comes from is how they already know how to be a lover to their spouse.

Inside our heart of hearts we already know the long-ings of our spouse. We already know what makes our spouse feel uniquely loved by us. We already know how to be a great lover to our spouse.

> Inside our heart of hearts we already know the longings of our spouse.

When my ministry couple got done reading their list, both of them were blown away by two things. First, how completely accurate their spouse already had the map inside of them to be their lover. Second, how well they knew to be a lover to their spouse but they just weren't doing it.

We had a great chat about both of these points, so I want to share this with you as well. The first ah-ha moment they had was about how well their spouse accurately knew how to be a lover to them. They were at one time your lover. They weren't just courting you philosophically. They were remember-ing from history. They remember through dating how they facilitated you falling in love with them. They were remembering the kindness, patience, and grace they gave to you as you shared your heart, experience, and flaws with them. They remember how you liked cards, gifts, a passionate kiss, and fun activities together.

They also remember the bruises they caused you in marriage and what helped you or brought you back to be engaged in your relationship. They've successfully wooed you several times even after marriage. They know how to be a lover to you. Their heart knows how to love your heart.

Like me with Lisa, you were made to be their lover. God created you in a unique way to have the specific type of patience they need to feel loved. You were made with unlimited creativity and intuitiveness to express kindness specifically toward your spouse. You were made for this journey divinely and specifically.

{ *God created you in a unique way to have the specific type of patience they need to feel loved.* }

The more I embrace my calling by the Father to love and serve Lisa, the easier it is to stay in the lover-spouse mode. I believe you were created for this ministry to love your spouse as much as you were created to parent your children (if you have them) or preform your ministry or vocation.

I find that when you're in your calling there's a sense of ease and confidence that comes as you practice your gifts. Practice, practice, practice!

Let's discuss the next obvious question. If they or I know in my heart of hearts how to be a great lover, then why in the world are we not being great lover spouses to our spouse? Well, let's look at some possible reasons for this amazing distance between what we know in our heart and what's actually showing up in our marriage.

I want to walk through five road blocks that can keep you from becoming a great lover-spouse. None of these road blocks are permanent road blocks. They may be issues you have yet to address. I've had some of these issues and I've worked with clients with multiple or all of these issues and have still seen them

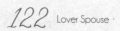

bravely address them to become awesome lover-spouses.

These roadblocks are not joint roadblocks. Rather they're individual roadblocks that you might need to address. However, it is very normal for each person in a marriage to have to slay these personal dragon's to be a better lover-spouse. As we go through these five major roadblocks, identify your own and make it your objective to aggressively address these to become the awesome lover-spouse God designed you to be.

This section may take some reflection and self-honesty, but it could really be valuable if you discover a particular roadblock that has kept you from being an awesome lover-spouse.

In my book *Upgrade Your Sex Life,* I address the first four of these so I'll quickly lay these out for you to assess.

 Abuse

You might have grown up with very good, even Godly, Christian parents, had pretty good friends, and gone through the normal bumps in life but life was good. You knew you were loved and safe your entire childhood. Sadly, this is not everyone's story. Many have experienced all types of traumatic events or abuses when growing up.

Some of us were physically abused and hit intensely without any purpose. Some were physically neglected growing up, and didn't receive the medical attention or other help they needed. Immature, addicted, or mood disordered parents might have inflicted emotional abuse or neglect. Yelling, shaming, and falsely accusing, can damage souls if this was the environment in which you grew up. As children and adolescents you may have been neglected emotionally and unable to be honest or share feelings in the home or weren't supported in aspects of your uniqueness (another form of neglect).

Sexual abuse is another huge problem and can impact up to 30 percent of women and 15 percent of men. Sexual abuse can especially have a wide variety of impacts on its survivors—feelings of worthlessness, shame, fear, lack of trust, over-compensation, over-performing, over-giving (in relationships), poor boundaries, or rigid boundaries.

Sexual abuse can affect the sexuality of victims as well. They might react to the trauma by being hypersexual with themselves or others. They might also suffer diminished desire for sex or lose their desire entirely as a reaction to this trauma. Sexual abuse can impact one's ability to connect emotionally with their spouse. The abuse survivor might go into a disconnected blank space or fantasy state during sex.

Sexual neglect can also happen to a child or adolescent growing up. In such cases they are given no sexual information—not on body changes, the meaning of sex, relational ideas involving sex, or standards for sexuality. Since they have no ideas about the act of sex or meaning of sex for themselves, they experience quite a range of impacts, depending on their first sexual encounter.

Abuse or neglect can impact people very differently. And many people have done well in working through their abuse or neglect issues. Those who have had these experiences and have not sifted through the issues related to them can encounter roadblocks. They may be limited in giving their sexuality or receiving their spouse's sexuality both inside and outside the bedroom.

 ## Addiction

This roadblock to the best lover-spouse is one not as widely thought of as the abuse roadblock, but it can definitely affect your marriage at a very deep level. If you're addicted to anything— alcohol, drugs, sex, pornography, food, gambling, entertainment, social media, work, ministry and so on— it robs you of emotional, spiritual, and moral development. I've worked with thousands of addicts in my center and this is so true.

Regardless of age—thirty, forty, fifty, sixty, or any other—the addicted person will reason and emote like a 13- to 15-year-old. He or she faces great challenges when trying to define a clear sense of right or wrong, or in taking responsibility for his or her behavior. He or she lives in a fantasy, a world in which an individual can do as he or she pleases, without any consequences.

All addictions negatively affect marriage to some degree. I can't tell you how many of my addicted clients have gone into recovery, and even a month in, began having the best marriage of their lives. They were able to move from an immature, object-function-type of a relationship into a mature, connected, relationship with their spouse.

Sex addiction is one addiction I've specialized in treating for more than thirty years now. This addiction brings its own unique set of difficulties for the addict and his or her spouse. As with other addictions, it robs the person of emotional, spiritual, and moral development. Sex addiction comes with added layers of secrecy and shame, which limits his or her ability to be authentic inside or outside the bedroom. It has an increasing distraction element to it that insidiously steals from the marriage or relationship. Hours of pornography, masturbation, sexting others, or arranging sexual hook-ups or relationships with others become huge impediments to a great marriage.

Also, all the sexual conditioning and comparing create dissatisfaction or false expectations that can definitely impact the sexuality of a marriage. The impact of betrayal on the partner also becomes an issue in the marriage when one is a sex addict. When one spouse lies about his or her behavior on a regular basis it impacts the marriage and sexuality of the couple. The impact of getting a sexually-transmitted disease (STD) is also a factor when the sex addicted partner engages in sexual contact with other people. The threat of job loss, financial loss, and one's reputation taking a hit can also be factors in marital challenges. Regardless of type, addictions impact who we are entirely. Immaturity in the addicted spouse causes multiple direct and indirect impacts on the marriage.

You might want to know the general characteristics of addiction to assess whether you or your partner have an addiction. If you feel you do, get help so you can be healthier and have a great marriage.

In the field of psychology, we use a diagnostic statistical manual (DSM) to identify disorders. The DSM criteria explains in clear terms the characteristics for addiction.

Addictions usually include any three of the following characteristics:

1. Do more of something for a longer period of time than expected.

2. Unsuccessful attempts to reduce or stop the behavior.

3. Spends a great deal of time acquiring or recovering from the behavior.

4. Behavior affects social or work life.

5. Reducing or not participating in normal social, occupational, or recreational activity to pursue the behavior.

6. Continuing to do the behavior knowing that it has caused problems.

7. A marked tolerance for the behavior (mean-

ing it takes more to get the same effect).

8. Withdrawal symptoms if not doing the behavior.

9. Doing the behavior to avoid withdrawal symptoms.

Now there's no way I'm going to talk to you about addictions being a roadblock for you to be an awesome lover-spouse and leave you in some variety of despair. Think back to how old you were thirty years ago. Seriously grab a snapshot of yourself in junior high, high school, college, or in your 30s.

I've seen people since that time over thirty years ago break and stay free from any and all the addictions mentioned. I've been personally free from sexual addiction for more than 30 years plus years. I've seen thousands of men and women work hard to heal their addictions so they could be a more mature spouse.

If you have personal addiction issues, start by getting honest. Then get accountable to someone of the same gender. I also recommend you get several books on the topic you struggle with and build a team or go to a support group so you can be free.

Christ died for our freedom from anything. If this is you, be hopeful He is with you through this personal journey. This journey alone can have a huge impact on you, your marriage, and your generation so go for it!

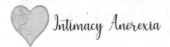 ## Intimacy Anorexia

I'm not talking about food anorexia here, in which one starves oneself or becomes addicted to doing so. What I want to share with you can be a huge roadblock to being a lover-spouse. Please read through this section. Not only for yourself but for those around you. I know many Christian couples who have struggled with Intimacy Anorexia but didn't have any information. You might be who God uses to point someone else down the path and help them get on the road to a much better marriage.

What I'm about to share with you is something I uncovered working with couples who felt married and alone. The pain of living with someone with Intimacy Anorexia is huge. If you see yourself or your spouse over the next few pages that can be a great beginning to understanding what's keeping you both from an awesome marriage.

Intimacy anorexia is the active withholding of emotional, spiritual, or sexual intimacy from one's spouse. Everyone else might view the person as warm and wonderful, however, the starved partner feels alone, disconnected, often unnoticed, or even unwanted in his or her relationship with the intimacy anorexic.

Below are the characteristics of intimacy anorexia:

Busy
The first characteristic of the intimacy anorexic is being so busy that he or she has little time for the spouse. This is a very common characteristic of most intimacy anorexics.

"Busy" can take on so many forms it could be a book all by itself. In the absence of connecting, "busy" becomes a type of avoidance intimacy anorexics actually employ to withhold intimacy—or even the potential for intimacy.

Compare this to a lover-spouse who is looking to get time with you. The lover-spouse wants and plans for dates, weekends together and just time to be together.

Blame

Blame is an Intimacy Anorexic characteristic that's nearly universal. When an issue or problem arises in the marriage, the anorexic first blames or puts responsibility for it on his or her spouse before becoming cognizant he or she contributed to the problem or issue. As you understand Intimacy Anorexia better, you'll learn that an Intimacy Anorexic wants to be in the "good box" all the time, and find it undesirable to be flawed, irresponsible, thoughtless, careless, or bad or even simply a flawed human being.

Blaming is almost reflexive for many Intimacy

Anorexics. It can be amazing to observe how much the emotional survival of the anorexic is at stake if he or she is found to be flawed, like the rest of us. Often, they can't face their intentional withholding. They don't see that starving their spouses directly affects the behavior they receive back from their spouse. They have a challenge seeing their behavior impacting their marriage.

Withholding Love

The Intimacy Anorexic often has a difficult time perceiving the intangible nature of withholding love. To withhold love is to not give your spouse love the way you know to do, or how they have asked to be loved. Each one of us wants to be loved, yet we all experience love in many different ways. Your spouse may want emotional sharing, long walks, a thoughtful note, or gift that says, "I was thinking of you." Some just want help around the house or with the children. Your partner needs to be shown love. The anorexic already knows how his or her spouse wants to be loved but withholds it.

Withholding Praise

The withholding of praise is also a significant recurring behavior for Intimacy Anorexics. To withhold praise is to refuse to share with your spouse what you view as his or her positive qualities as a person and positive impact on your life. You can see how this would be in contrast to a lover-spouse who can't stop praising their spouse even for little things.

All of us have amazing, positive qualities. Over time, Intimacy Anorexics ceases this positive vision of the spouse and tend to focus on the flaws of one's partner. If you haven't been praising your spouse regularly for who he or she is and what he or she does, may I suggest that you could be actively and intentionally not praising them.

Withholding Sex

By far, of all the behavioral characteristics of Intimacy Anorexia, withholding of sex is probably the easiest to measure, and at the very least, most obvious. Withholding sex from one's spouse is anything one does to avoid having sex, including sabotaging sexual encounters or not connecting emotionally during sex.

You can tell if you're the spouse or the Intimacy Anorexic by recalling the last time you had sex. It might not be as easy for the anorexic to remember the last time he or she sabotaged a sexual encounter, whether it was before, during, or after it. It's even harder for the anorexic to remember withholding emotionally and spiritually during sex, or of giving all of himself or herself to his or her spouse. Any of these behaviors could be an example of withholding sex. (In the *Intimacy Anorexia: The Workbook*, I give some of these examples):

- During sex, do you look at your spouse or close your eyes?
- Do you think of other things to do during sex?
- Do you fantasize about others or porn during sex?
- Do you communicate positively during sex?
- Are you silent during sex?
- Do you act as if you dread sex?

- Do you hurry your spouse to get it over with?
- Do you leave your spouse emotionally or physically after sex?
- Do you shut your spouse down when talking about sex?
- Do you make your spouse initiate all the sex?
- As a spouse you feel empty or alone during sex
- Any sexual creativity is shamed or silenced

A lover-spouse wants sex. A lover is not looking for how to get out of sex but looking for times to be sexual. A lover-spouse wants to hear the reasonable desires of the spouse. A lover-spouse enjoys employing creativity during sex just for the pleasure of giving pleasure.

Withholding Spiritually

The characteristic of withholding spiritually is also only noticed by the spouse. I've had clients that were spiritual leaders, pastors, rabbis, and even medicine men who didn't connect spiritually with their spouses. To withhold spiritually is to withhold spiritual connectedness from one's spouse—regardless of faith practices (or lack thereof)— so there's no genuine, spiritually connective behavior with him or her. The anorexic might be religious to the hilt, but the spirituality isn't authentic in the presence of his or her spouse.

I've heard countless excuses for this, especially from the religious anorexic, (regardless of faith): "I do this just by myself." "It's not my personality." "My partner is too spiritual (or not spiritual enough), so I don't connect with him or her, spiritually." Regardless of the rationalization, there's an absence of spiritual connection between the Intimacy Anorexic and his or her spouse. A lover-spouse wants to connect spiritually and do so consistently.

Feelings

This characteristic can be described as being unwilling or unable to share feelings with one's spouse. Having difficulty sharing feelings is also a universal characteristic of the Intimacy Anorexic. As we stated earlier, addictions hinder emotional development.

If you're the spouse of an Intimacy Anorexic, you may have difficulty remembering a time when your husband or wife voluntarily shared feelings with you without having to write the "emotional check" for the experience. If the Intimacy Anorexic's image of the marriage is threatened, or he or she really blows it some-how, you can expect some feelings being shared but this fades away a week or two after the activating event.

The sharing of feelings is an act of authenticity that can be scary, difficult, or both, for the Inti-macy Anorexic. The anorexic's unwillingness or inability to share feelings can be intentional, to not give you love the way he or she knows you like it. At some point, this could legitimately be a skill deficit.

If you or your spouse are really challenged in the emotional area, I strongly recommend the book *Emotional Fitness.* This book walks you through a regimen to actually connect and feel feelings as well as be able to share your feel-ings.

The lover-spouse wants to know how their spouse feels. The lover-spouse is sensitive to shifts in their spouse's moods. The lover-spouse has the patience to hear feelings as the desire to discover what's on their wonderful spouse's heart. Sharing feelings can be a fun part of being married to your favorite person.

Criticism

Ongoing or ungrounded criticism that leads to distance in the marriage is the seventh characteristic of intimacy anorexia. This can include low-grade put-downs toward one's partner, focusing on what he or she does wrong, or just regularly criticizing his or her bad ideas. Ungrounded criticism has little to do with reality. This strategy may be used to push the spouse away or throw him or her off the trail of something. Either way, it intentionally creates distance.

Criticism in this category doesn't need to be spoken. So many have told me that their husbands or wives don't actually verbalize their criticism, but they can feel it constantly anyway.

If criticism is an active strategy, the Intimacy Anorexic will be much faster at making a list of what's wrong, defective, or weak about their spouse than what is amazing. Criticism can also be employed as a tactic to push away one's partner when intimacy or sex seems to be expected. This would include: birthdays, holidays, and right before vacation. This is the Intimacy Anorexic pushing the partner away so he or she doesn't have to give to the partner emotionally or sexually.

As a potential lover-spouse you can quickly evaluate your words of praise versus your words of criticism over the last week, month or year. To go deep, evaluate your thoughts about your spouse when you're alone or driving. Do they tend to drift more toward criticism or praise?

Anger/Silence

My experience with Intimacy Anorexics is that not all use silence or anger as characteristic of their Intimacy Anorexia. However, those who use anger or silence as a characteristic do so with a vengeance. This Intimacy Anorexia characteristic is described as any use of anger or silence to push away, punish, or control one's spouse.

I've spent countless hours listening to stories from spouses and Intimacy Anorexics alike about using anger or silence toward their spouse. Sometimes the examples are extreme, including times when the Intimacy Anorex- ic won't talk to his or her spouse for days or weeks—even while living in the same house. The anger explosion is often over something minor and is a great tool to push the partner away and avoid giving one's heart to them.

Here the lover-spouse would of course have anger. Lover-spouses would be in pain to be silent especially to punish. You can again look over the years to see if you've used anger or silence to create or maintain distance in your marriage.

Money

The characteristic of controlling or shaming one's spouse about money is probably the least common among Intimacy Anorexics. However, those who employ this use it with an iron fist. Most of the anorexics who control or shame with money do so by keeping their spouses ignorant of household finances, give them an allowance, make their spouses ask for money, or refuse to allow their spouse to have a credit card or checkbook.

However, there is another side of controlling through money. I call it "controlling through abundance." This spouse, male or female, has substantial money, but has many controls over it. Their attitude is, I buy you everything, so don't complain about a lack of intimacy, love, or sex. This type of controlling by money isn't as obvious as control by not giving.

Roommate

The spouse of the anorexic feels like (or even states it out loud) a roommate. I've heard this comment from spouses so many times that I often add it to the end of my assessment of clients for anorexia.

When you feel like a roommate to your spouse,

the feelings of alone, unchosen, unwanted, confused and hurt. are ongoing. The pain of aloneness over time can have impacts on your health and general outlook on life. This alone feeling can also move you toward over-functioning or medicating in some manner. If you or your spouse are experiencing this, Intimacy Anorexia might be keeping you from having a great marriage.

In the box below, I've placed each one of these characteristics for you to score for yourself. In the first column circle yes or no about how you feel this characteristic applies to you.

Then go to the second column and guess how your spouse would answer concerning whether you have the characteristic. Last, allow your spouse to answer these yes or no questions about yourself.

Characteristic	As I'd Respond	As I Think My Partner Would Respond	My Partner's Response
Busy	Y N	Y N	Y N

Blame	Y N	Y N	Y N
Withholding Love	Y N	Y N	Y N
Withholding Praise	Y N	Y N	Y N
Withholding Sex	Y N	Y N	Y N
Withholding Spiritually	Y N	Y N	Y N
Feelings	Y N	Y N	Y N
Criticism	Y N	Y N	Y N
Anger/Silence	Y N	Y N	Y N
Money	Y N	Y N	Y N
Roommate	Y N	Y N	Y N

If you answered yes to five or more questions, Intimacy Anorexia is most likely present in your relationship. There is hope! Intimacy Anorexia can go into full remission. Over the years, I've helped numerous clients who hadn't had sex for ten years or more due to Intimacy Anorexia. Often, within six to eight weeks of developing intimacy skills, these clients not only began having the best sex of their lives, but both spouses actually started liking each other again.

Regardless of your battlefield (i.e., sexual abuse, addiction, or Intimacy Anorexia) you can become a great lover-spouse. I've counseled men and women from all walks of life with these issues— some with all three— and have seen their sex lives make an incredible turnaround.

What follows below is an outline of a very practical non-touchy-feely approach for overcoming each one of these battlefronts. In my counseling practice, I've assisted my clients in winning these battles thousands of times. The outline works if you do the work that needs to be done.

You may not have any of these challenges to work through. If you don't, be thankful! You might just want to glance through this section for general information, though, because these issues are very prevalent in our church today, so you may be able to pass on some help to someone else I'll never get the opportunity to meet.

♥ Resolving Abuse

Regardless of the gender of your perpetrator, or the age difference, the following exercises can help tremendously in overcoming abuse issues. It will help you gain closure for past painful events. In case you need more help than afforded by these two exercises, seek the guidance of a professional counselor who specializes in healing the abuse that has happened to you or your spouse.

♥ Symbolic Confrontation

Realize that when you experienced abuse, all of you—entirely—was affected. Even if you didn't want to be, you were greatly traumatized. Moreover, when someone is sexual, they're absolutely the most vulnerable they can be. So if a sexual perpetrator uses you as a sex object, it affected you in all three parts of your being (spirit, soul, and body). Physical and emotional abuse impacts you significantly as well.

Not all, but many traditional therapists are in-effective in handling abuse because they try to deal with this three-dimensional problem using a one-dimensional method. The process I'm about to outline engages all three parts of your woundedness.

Note: As a word of caution, before you start the symbolic confrontations, if you have heart trouble or other health issues, first consult your physician before attempting any of this work.

Prepare your offenders list–Write a list of the offender(s) in your life. List the offenses they committed, your age at the time of each of-fense, and a brief description of the offense.

Example:
- When I was seven years old, a neighbor boy had me...
- Dad left me when I was nine.
- A female babysitter forced me, at age twelve, to...
- A stranger...

Rank these offenses in order of intensity, with the number "1" identifying the offense in which the highest level of abuse experienced. Next, you'll confront each perpetrator **symbolically**, one at a time (an explanation of how to do this follows). You'll symbolically confront one person per day, starting with the worst offender. I usually recommend that you give yourself 1-3 days between confronting each perpetrator.

Symbolic confrontations have four components that are all very important:

1. Write your anger letter.
2. Read your letter out loud.
3. Warm up for your symbolic confrontation.
4. Carry out your symbolic confrontation (hit the target).

I will detail each step below. Before starting, turn your phone off and make sure you have complete privacy for your confrontation.

1. Anger Letter —Write down the name of your offender, if you know it, and then write him

or her a letter expressing all your feelings. **Do not mail the letter**— it's strictly therapeutic for your own healing. If you could put this person in a chair, strap them down, and gag them, what would you like to say to them regarding what they have done to you? Include in your letter how his or her actions affected your life, your relationships, and your sexuality. Don't hold back any thoughts or feelings, and don't worry about your expression, either. More than likely, abuse has dramatically affected your life. Your perpetrators deserve the rage you feel about them.

2. Read the Letter Aloud—Read your letter as if to your offender. This is an important part of the exercise as well. As you read the letter, feelings will swell up inside of you. This is normal. The next step will help discharge that trauma.

3. Warm Up—Get a racquet or padded bat (usually available wherever bats are sold). You'll also need a mattress, pillow, or punching bag. Using your bat, strike the mattress with small, medium, large, and extra-large hits. Practice doing this a time or two. Also, warm up your voice by

saying "no" with each hit, louder and louder. Although this may seem awkward at first, it's essential to your symbolic confrontation, which will enable you to release your rage.

4. Hit the Target—Now go at it with your padded bat on the mattress. Really let that mattress have it (as it symbolizes your perpetrator). You can hit, yell, kick, or do whatever you need to do to get the rage, shame, and hate out of you, and back on your perpetrator where it belongs. It's their shame you have been carrying all these years, not yours. This last step can take anywhere from ten minutes to an hour, depending on the ordeal you experienced and how deeply the pain is lodged inside of you. The more emotion you let out, the better you will feel afterward. You're now taking the bullet out of your being—spirit, soul, and body—and giving it back to the person responsible for inflicting you with it.

This is how a symbolic confrontation takes place. I've personally done this exercise with each of the offenders in my life. This gave me a concrete place and time for when I pulled the bullets out of my soul and began to heal.

I've noticed that everyone's experience with symbolic confrontation is quite unique. Some feel different immediately afterward. For others, it takes a few days before they realize they are free of the bondage that once strangled them.

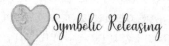 Symbolic Releasing

In this second step you will not address your anger. Instead, you will release yourself from the perpetrator. You may have heard it said that forgiveness is more for you than for anyone else. My personal and professional experience concurs with that after doing the symbolic releasing—forgiveness is very therapeutic.

In this exercise you'll need two chairs and privacy. Again, turn off the phone and make sure everyone is out of the house. Turn two chairs to face each other. There are three phases to this exercise. I'll walk you through each one.

Phase 1—Sit in one of the chairs (chair A). From that seat you'll role-play the perpetrator. You can use your perpetrator's name if you know it. If he or she was a stranger, you can give him or her a name or simply say, "I am the one who abused you."

Acting as the perpetrator ("Fred" in this exercise), face chair B. Imagine yourself sitting in chair B. As Fred, you can own the abuse, apologize, and ask for forgiveness. Be sure to acknowledge the costs to yourself—the victim. Be specific and don't just say, "I'm sorry." Instead, if Fred was an adult who forced you into sex as a child, you may say something like, "I am the one who made you perform sex. I used you like other boys I had victimized. You were just an object to me when I did this to you. I know I must have damaged your life. I hope you can heal. I now ask you to forgive me."

Phase 2—After the perpetrator has appropriately apologized to you, then physically get up and move to chair B. In chair B, role-play yourself receiving the information from your perpetrator, just role-played. You've just heard him apologize and ask forgiveness for the acts he did to you, and the effect they had on you.

In chair B, you can respond *any way you like.* You may not be ready to release the offender at this time. Whatever your thoughts or feelings are, verbalize them out loud to the perpetrator. The purpose of this exercise is for you to be honest. Releasing the offender at some point is a gift you can give to yourself. His or her life moved on, whether you "let them off the hook" or not. By forgiving and releasing the offender, you're **not** approving of what he or she did to you. You are simply releasing that behavior from having an influence in your life any longer.

If you are unable to forgive or release the offender at this time, try this exercise again in a month or so. However, if you were able to let go, move on to Phase 3.

Phase 3—Physically move back to chair A and resume the role of the perpetrator. Now you need to respond to the forgiveness or releasing that has been extended toward you. This concludes your symbolic confrontation. Fred would say something like, "I don't deserve your forgiveness, but thank you for forgiving me. I hope you can live free from the pain I caused you."

This is a powerful exercise for most people. As you complete it, you can fully say goodbye to this chapter of your life.

From this point on, at least for the majority of people who complete this exercise, you'll be able to view the abuse as part of your history, but no longer suffer the effects of it. This is similar to bearing a scar from an accident, but no longer suffering the pain of it.

I hope that all who need to heal from the lingering effects of abuse will complete these exercises. They have changed thousands of men's and women's lives. If you still struggle with the impact of sexual trauma after doing these exercises, I recommend you see a counselor who specializes in sexual trauma. You deserve to be free and move toward being a great lover-spouse.

Overcoming Addiction

Overcoming an addiction can be one of the hardest, but most life-changing things someone can do in life. The grip of addiction is real, and so are the principles for healing. Here are some general points on addiction, and a few suggestions for those who struggle with sexual addiction.

- You have to be honest that you have a problem.
- You have to be willing to take full responsibility for the problem. (I tell my clients, "When you're the problem, you're the solution.")
- Educate yourself about your particular addictions.
- Get into a Twelve Step support group or addiction recovery group specific to your issue.
- Call someone from that group every day for at least ninety days.
- Get a sponsor in the group.
- Get professional help if you are failing.
- Focus on the positive you are fighting for.

These sex addiction suggestions are taken from the books, *The Final Freedom: Pioneering Sexual Addiction* and, *101 Freedom Exercises for Sexual Addiction*. I recommend the sex addict do all the above and consider these ideas as well:

Block all access to the behavior (i.e., a porn blocker, quit social media, etc.).

Set consequences for acting out behavior (i.e., pick up trash for two hours).

- If the addiction involved others, break off all contact with them.
- Do an assessment to find out what type of sex addict you are. (There is a test available at www.sexaddict.com, or call a counselor trained by www.aasat.org
- Make arrangements to do a three- or five-day intensive in our office.
- Consider doing quarterly polygraphs to verify freedom sobriety and re-establish trust.
- Educate yourself of the impact on your partner (i.e., *Helping Her Heal* DVD, *Partners: Healing from His Addiction* book available at www.drdougweiss.com).

♥ Healing Intimacy Anorexia

Intimacy Anorexia is its own process of healing and recovery. Much like the addiction suggestions, get educated (*Intimacy Anorexia: The Book, Intimacy Anorexia: The Workbook, Intimacy Anorexia: The Steps,* as well as our *Married and Alone* series). Joining a telephone group for Intimacy Anorexia, and doing a three or five-day intensive with us could be very helpful to you.

In this book we'll discuss what we call the three dailies (two feelings, two praises, and spiritual connection). These are great for every relationship, but imperative for Intimacy Anorexia. The Intimacy Anorexic should take full responsibility to initiate these exercises and give himself or herself a consequence if the activities haven't been initiated by a certain time each day. For example, if Sue is the Intimacy Anorexic, she would initiate. She would set a 9 p.m. deadline for completing the dailies, and if not completed, she would give John a thirty-minute massage, starting at 9:01 p.m.

For the first sixty days, the Intimacy Anorexic initiates all sexual encounters. He or she would set consequences for not doing so. So, if Tony is the Intimacy Anorexic, he would ask Jan to be sexual, with an agreed upon frequency each week. If these goals aren't met, he would give himself a consequence (i.e., clean toilets, sleep in garage, or give $100 to the political party he doesn't vote for).

Regardless of the roadblock you may have, there's always hope if you're honest and willing to do the work. I've worked with men and women who had one of three, two of three, and all three roadblocks we covered so far. They did the work and now have amazingly healthy marriages.

You may need to face and overcome your roadblock. Decide for yourself what you need to do to have an amazing marriage.

Regardless of the roadblock you
may have, there's always hope if
you're honest and willing to
do the work.

Family of Origin

You might have come from a great healthy Christian family. You saw two people loving and serving each other. You saw problems being addressed on a consistent basis. You heard them praise one another and witnessed them being affectionate with one another. You didn't see a lot of arguing. Instead, you saw health and happiness. You were immersed in these patterns growing up and they became your default behaviors in a marriage, especially stress. You may have had great examples of marriage from your family of origin, patient, kind, respectful, even under stressful periods in the marriage.

In the space provided, write out some of the strengths and weaknesses you saw in your parents individually and what systems existed in their marriage. A system is how things worked or didn't work in their marriage; Example: One person makes decisions, they paid bills together, they saved or didn't save money, were active in church, sat in front of the television for hours a day, etc. I'll also add stepdad and stepmom relationships as well. If this applies to you, take the time to fill their information out as well.

Dad (What I learned about marriage)

His strengths in marriage were:

1. _____
2. _____
3. _____
4. _____
5. _____
6. _____

His weakness in marriage were:

1. _____
2. _____
3. _____
4. _____
5. _____
6. _____

Mom (What I learned about marriage)

Her strengths in marriage were:

1._____
2._____
3._____
4._____
5._____
6._____

Her weakness in marriage were:

1._____
2._____
3._____
4._____
5._____
6._____

Step Dad (What I learned about marriage)

His strengths in marriage were:

1._____
2._____
3._____
4._____
5._____
6._____

His weakness in marriage were:

1._____
2._____
3._____
4._____
5._____
6._____

Step Mom (What I learned about marriage)

Her strengths in marriage were:

1._____
2._____
3._____
4._____
5._____
6._____

Her weakness in marriage were:

1._____
2._____
3._____
4._____
5._____
6._____

Some of the systems I saw in my
parent's marriage that worked were:

1._____
2._____
3._____
4._____
5._____
6._____
7._____
8._____
9._____
10._____

Some of the systems I saw in my parent's marriage that didn't worked were:

1. _____
2. _____
3. _____
4. _____
5. _____
6. _____
7. _____
8. _____
9. _____
10. _____

I could write a whole book on what I learned from my mom and dad in marriage. However, the point is that you can see you might have picked up some bad or good from your family of origin.

I want to be clear you've already outgrown your parents in other areas of your life. You might have become more financially successful; more educated; more Godly; healthier physically or emotionally; more mature; less addicted; less critical and so on. My point is you've already outgrown your parents in some manner so you can outgrow any less than healthy example or system in their marriage to become an amazing lover-spouse.

Take some time to reflect what you gleaned from writing these strengths/weaknesses and systems you experienced growing up. When you feel you have something of value to share from this exercise, share it with your spouse. If you need to make some goals after looking at this then feel free to do that so you can be a great lover-spouse.

My point is you've already out-grown your parents in some manner so you can outgrow any less than healthy example or system in their marriage to become an amazing lover-spouse.

Sin

As a psychologist I am always amazed at my Christian colleagues who want to psychobabble or make something an "issue." One thing that keeps you from becoming a great lover-spouse is just plain sin.

Sin is something you've been convicted of by the Holy Spirit—that you're doing wrong and you keep doing it. That is one area of sin. You unconsciously think or behave as, "I know it's wrong but too bad I don't want to change." This type of sin is when you handle yourself in a willful way to not address a known behavior or relationship that is unhealthy in your life. My experience is when we get this attitude of willfulness in an area of our life it affects our heart. The impact on our heart—guilt, shame, secrecy, rebellion—will impact us in our marriage.

The other area of sin is found in James 4:17: "Anyone, then, who knows the good he ought to do and doesn't do it, sins." This is a powerful scripture when it comes to marriage. Earlier I had you write out "If I was your lover I would..." You already know the good to do toward your spouse. Your heart already has a clear roadmap to love your spouse. You not doing it is sin. Not just sin against your spouse but sin against your Father-in-law, God.

How we treat our spouse is a big issue to God. So, sin is different than abuse, addiction, anorexia, and family of origin issues. These you identify or work your way through to become an awesome lover-spouse.

With sin you have to acknowledge to God and your spouse and repent. When you repent you verbally ask forgiveness and make a plan to change your behavior. Having accountability with a same gender person can keep you from going back to your sin.

{ *How we treat our spouse is a big issue to God.* }

If this is your issue, you already know it is. In the space below, identify any sin you know you have in the way you behave or believe (attitude) about your spouse:

My sins would be:

_____
_____
_____
_____
_____
_____
_____
_____
_____
_____
_____

If you identified some sins, I encourage you to take

the following three steps. First, confess in a real way these sins to God. He already knows and He wants to release the grace to you to overcome these patterns of sin in your life.

Second, confess your sin to your spouse. In most cases they already know how you sin against them. The scripture says in James 5:16, "Therefore confess your sins to each other and pray for each other so you may be healed." This will require some humility, but it can set a new trajectory for you in your marriage. An honest sin can be healed. A covered sin tends to grow or multiply in our life.

> An honest sin can be healed. A covered sin tends to grow or multiply in our life.

I've been married well over thirty years as I write these pages. I can remember several times I had to repent to Lisa for attitudes or behaviors. Sometimes there were ways I was thinking, believing or behaving toward her. Other times the sin had nothing to do with her directly.

I have a gracious, Godly wife. She would forgive me every time. I can remember time and time again if I confessed to Lisa, my sin stopped occurring. We all deserve to have the scripture work in our lives. But we need to do what it says for it to work in our lives.

Third, make a plan to connect this sin pattern or belief and get accountable to someone of the same gender on a weekly basis. I find anything I'm accountable for evaporates from my life.

I'll give you a non-marriage example. Throughout my life I've written books on planes and hotel rooms when I traveled. Over the last year or so I was traveling less and not writing as much. The Spirit convicted me that I needed to get back to writing and to start with this book you're reading.

I went into my staff meeting and asked which therapist was newest to our group. They identified themselves and I said I'll be accountable to you by next week to write a chapter and if I don't, I'll give you one hundred dollars. Needless to say, I started to write and thus far I haven't paid anyone. I knew to do good (write), I responded to God and my peers, got accountable and I've been writing ever since (healed).

Sin can keep you from being an amazing lover-spouse. Don't let this stop you, go determinedly into repentance and heal you so you can be the lover-spouse Christ has empowered you to be.

Sin can keep you from being an amazing lover-spouse.

Sacred Intimacy

Here we come to a critical delineation between a functional spouse and a lover-spouse. The bedroom of our relationship is the most sacred of places for a married couple.

The bedroom is the place where we do forsake all others. We close the door to all of our day, our responsibility, and we shed our clothes and we're, "Naked, and they felt no shame" (Genesis 2:25).

In the bedroom, we're spiritually, emotionally, physically and sexually naked before our spouse and our God. Sex is a place of vulnerability and pleasure. This is an endless place to play as lovers. We can share until death do us part.

However, I counsel Christians every week in the areas of sex. I'm amazed at how little they know about sex from a theological and biological perspective. I've written several books about sex or chapters in books about sex.

Let me share with you a few of these titles because this is an area of that lover-spouse Christians need real information for their personal life.

Sex, Men and God
Upgrade Your Sex Life
Clean
Lust Free Living
Best Sex for Men DVD
Best Sex for Women DVD
Intimacy: A 100 Day Guide to Lasting Relationships
The Final Freedom
Intimacy Anorexia
Born for War (Young Men) DVD
Princes Take Longer Than Frogs (Young Women)
Steps to Sexual Health DVD Series (Young Girls)

As you can see God has used me for decades to share the good news about sex and help churches and couples have a better understanding and better sex life. I believe Christ wants us to be excellent lovers sexually to our spouses. I'm also aware of the abuse, trauma, addiction, and anorexia that Christians experience sexually. Despite this trauma, they are able to work through the issues to also have a great sex life.

I would like this conversation to start where sexuality began, in the heart of God. God created sex, the devil didn't (he can't create anything). Before creation, God, in his timeless place thought through all of creation and our very specific creation to be in His image to multiply ourselves.

As I mentioned before, God created sex before Adam's creation. Go back and review the creation story. When God created the mammal animals, they were all commanded to "go forth and multiply." How do mammals multiply? They have sex. All the animals in the Garden of Eden had sex. The Garden of Eden was a sexual place before the fall and before Adam.

When God created Adam, he was made complete with all his sexuality, including body parts completely intact. Adam was a sexual being even though Eve was not yet created. Eve was also created as a sexual being in totality prior to being brought to Adam.

Adam and Eve were also sexual in the garden. Sex was part of God's plan. Sex was holy and preceded the fall. Sex was not a result of the Fall although sex continued after the Fall.

I learned a term in Bible school called "omnipresent." This term simply means that God is everywhere all the time. However, many Christians believe that God is everywhere all the time except when we're having sex. This is truly funny as if God leaves because we're being sexual.

Lover-spouses understand that sex is Godly, good, and fun. Lover-spouses look forward to and desire sexual encounter. Lover-spouses see the whole house as a place to have sexual encounters. Lover-spouses are comfortable and confident being sexual, expressing themselves sexually, creating sexual opportunities, being playful, and creating a positive inviting sexual environment.

{ *Lover-spouses understand that sex is Godly, good, and fun.* }

Some spouses have a journey to reclaim Christ in their sexuality. I've been sexually abused and many other Christians have had that attack on their sexuality to process through. I know many lover-spouses who have been through sexual trauma and refused to allow this to rob them of a great sex life. They have successfully worked through this, as I have.

Sexual addiction is a real situation in the body of Christ, mostly affecting men but also growing numbers of women. The addiction behavior includes pornography, self sex (masturbation), sex through technology, sex with others, sex services, etc. The results are the same. I've been free from sexual addiction for thirty-two years. I've seen many Christians get the help they needed to reclaim a healthy, connected sexuality and become great lover-spouses.

Intimacy Anorexia, as we discussed earlier, is another secret in the church robbing couples of a great sex life. Again, I've seen thousands take the journey to heal and they became intimate lover-spouses.

The sexually immature who can't talk about sex, initiate sex, want the lights off, and want to get it over as quickly as possible, live among the church as well.

They too get help from a same gender Christian counselor and can also mature into a great lover-spouse.

The self-conscious, self-absorbed also live among us. They can't stop thinking about their body appearance, their performance, which then limits their ability to engage and enjoy sex. They'll often try to influence the other person as well from fully engaging or being sexually creative.

Lover-spouses push through like super heroes on any issue. They greatly desire to become great sexual lovers. The functional spouse will often use their challenges as excuses not to grow. This self-inflicted choice can bring unmeasurable pain to the other spouse. The functional spouse will often have a less than "oh yeah" attitude toward sex. In their heart they've agreed with beliefs like:

- I have to have sex (not get to)
- It's a duty
- It's for them
- It's for procreation only
- It's a curse
- It's unnecessary

When the heart believes a lie, the results are true. I can't tell you the intellectual pain this idea creates for the spouse of rejection (i.e., feelings of not being good enough, feeling ugly, unwanted, used and unimportant.) These lies create cracks in the most sacred part of a marriage.

If you're both a lover-spouse, sexually receiving one another, engaging sexually, and creating time and places to enjoy each other then you're enjoying God's gift to you both. If one or both of you are using your challenges, immaturity, or self-absorption as an excuse to not be a lover-spouse, then pain will be in the marriage and pain always looks for a medicine.

 *Learning*

Sex is one of those areas of life like money, health, and parenting which are all lifelong learning experiences. You and your spouse will have a lifetime of sexually experiencing, discovering, and relearning about each other.

I like to share with my clients that there are two ways to learning or living for that matter. You can learn intentionally and practically or you can learn accidently and reactively.

I like learning practically and intentionally. I find it's cheaper to learn through a book, a friend, a mentor or even a class than it is to learn by life teaching me something.

You can learn about your spouse sexually either accidently or intentionally. It's totally acceptable to explore what pleasures each other. It's acceptable to ask questions about what feels pleasurable and what doesn't. It's acceptable to experiment as long as both people agree and no harm is being done to your lover.

However, I will give two absolute "nevers" surrounding sexuality. Never watch porn during sex, period. You can't watch porn and not lust after another person. Lust is sin and porn is never right for a Christian marriage. Second, no third person is ever acceptable in your sex life. This is adultery and is forbidden by God, period.

> { *Lust is sin and porn is never right for a Christian marriage.* }

If you want to learn about sexuality, I have a life-changing book about sexuality called *Upgrade Your Sex Life*. I explain to couples about their unique sexual expressions, how to utilize this knowledge during foreplay, during sex, and after sex. This book has taken many couples sex life to another level. There are secular books on sexuality, but I would avoid these. Go to a safe place like Christianbooks.com to search for Christian books on sexuality.

 ## Agreeing

In almost every area of marriage, it's best if we can agree on things to make that specific area of life easier. Some couples naturally flow sexually. They have established how frequently to have sex, what works for them sexually, and openly talk about sex.

However, in counseling Christians, I find the "flow" couple is more the exception than the rule. I want to discuss a few points to agree on sexually. If you feel you want more information, I really encourage you to read *Upgrade Your Sex Life*.

The first important point to agree on is how often you want to be sexual together. 1, 2, 3, 4, or 5 times a week? There is no wrong answer. Each couple needs to negotiate this point. Both of you could experience more peace just knowing and agreeing on how often you'll be enjoying sex together.

Second, agreeing on how to structure how often you want to have sex. You and your spouse can pick specific days, split the week up, or rotate days or weeks. This will help create a clear understanding to sexually agree upon.

Agreeing that both people initiate relatively equally can be important as well. Even if you never say no, if you never initiate then the other person sexually feels this and feels unequal, not prioritized, and unimportant.

The last thing to agree on is what is acceptable to you both sexually. Having an honest talk about acceptable positions and places/locations that you both fully agree to is also important. These are the colors you get to paint with sexually.

Being a sexual lover-spouse is our privilege. You should consider it an an awesome responsibility to connect to pleasure and be able to satiate like a lover-spouse. Sex is an amazing gift God has bestowed on us. Like all of His gifts, we're stewards of the gift. We can be awesome stewards or irresponsible, selfish stewards of our sexuality and how we express this toward our spouse.

I decided to be an awesome steward of my sexuality. I had to do some fighting to get healed, free, and healthy. I did the work well because Jesus died so I could. It's worth it to my marriage and to Lisa that I am a vibrant, healthy, and sexual lover-spouse.

You may have challenges, things to address, conversations to have but you have the time to become an awesome lover-spouse sexually. So, go for it!

You should consider it an an
awesome responsibility to connect
to pleasure and be able to satiate
like a lover-spouse.

P.I.C.K.

Being a lover is part of your history prior to marrying the love of your life. Being a lover wasn't forced on you, taught to you, or something you studied. Rather, being a lover was part of who you are. We were all lovers to some degree or another prior to marriage. For most of us, we were lovers to more than one person. When I use the term "lover," I'm not in any manner eluding it to sex or sexuality. I mean you were giving of yourself in some or several ways toward another that symbolized or meant "I love you, the way you want to be loved."

Some of us started being lovers in elementary school. By high school or early adulthood, most of us have experienced our share of highs and lows in regards to being a lover. As we all know too well, not all early relationships end in marriage but we were lovers still to those people and that's why those breakups were so painful and devastating for some of us.

In this chapter, I want to discuss four pretty clear characteristics of a lover. In these pages I want you to remember who you were in the past. You were a lover, you are a lover, and you will always be a lover. You can range from being a terrible lover to an amazing lover. The kind of lover you are to your spouse is up to you. As you think about these characteristics, you'll see how you have been a lover. Pay special attention to the memories that specifically apply to your spouse.

He or she is the one you promised to be a lover to until you or they die. These memories may be a helpful roadmap. It will give you some idea of the type of lover you currently are or at least give you some idea of where to go from here. You might need to reengage your spouse with ideas that you already know work well to make them feel loved by you.

 Reoccupied (P)

What do you think of when I say the preoccupied?

Perhaps words such as adrift, aloof, day dreaming, or unfocused come to mind? We can get preoccupied about sports (especially in certain regions in our country), politics, work, hobbies, technology, entertainment and apps. The world we currently live in provides ample opportunity to divide and distract our heart, mind, and emotions on any given day. However, when a lover is preoccupied with the one they love, it's really a different experience than being preoccupied about anything else in the universe.

When you're preoccupied with the one you love it's almost all-consuming. You wonder what they're doing, thinking, feeling or experiencing while at the same time you're working, in class, just doing chores or other activities. Then you become preoccupied with past conversations together, hugs, kisses, notes, or things you did together. You go into an almost timeless state reviewing the movie of your relationship and pushing pause to think and feel about this or that moment.

> *When you're preoccupied with the one you love it's almost all-consuming.*

Then there's the future preoccupation of what you'll do later today, next week, month, year, and so on. Your preoccupation with the one you love goes into thousands of directions—what they wore, how they smelled, what they did, how they smiled, how they touched you, the activities and people you interacted with together, what you learned about them, how they think and feel, how compatible they are to you, and how they complement you. They're amazing, wonderful and just thinking of them gives you a warm feeling.

Being preoccupied as a lover doesn't have to ever end. As a lover you look for the good, find it and ruminate on it constantly. If you stay a lover-spouse, preoccupation stays with you.

*Being preoccupied as a lover
doesn't have to ever end.*

Today I was on my way to the Denver airport, which is two hours away from my house. Often on this drive I think about the past, present, and future with Lisa. I think of things we have done or saw together, what I enjoy about her and what I look forward to doing when I get back.

The preoccupation switch can turn off in a marriage as responsibilities such as the house, car, neighbors, church, and children are added to life. These things can make you distracted. This functional couple can start to emphasize task instead of relationship. They become preoccupied over what needs to be done, not their lover. They focus on what needs to be paid, not their lover. They think about the weaknesses of their lover instead of their strengths.

This is easy to figure out. If I was to ask you make a list of your spouse's positive qualities how long would that take? If I was to ask you to make a list of your spouse's negative characteristics how long would that take? Whatever would take you the longest might be your focus.

Getting back your preoccupation for your spouse is like getting back into shape if you've put on a few pounds. If you've been in shape before you know the importance of getting cardio exercise back into your life. If you swim, hike, bike, run, play a sport or just hit that treadmill, you have to get back to actually doing that activity.

To remind yourself, you can put some of your thoughts and ideas into your phone or on sticky notes, or some other method. You'll need to set aside some time daily, just a few minutes. You can mentally go over a list while you are driving but it can limit the quality of your preoccupation, and for your sake and others, I want you focused on your driving. You can put a daily alarm on your phone and find a quiet place to close your eyes and think, feel, or imagine about you lover. Here are some thoughts to help you get back into the habit of being preoccupied with your lover again.

Thoughts:

- What I remember about first meeting my spouse?
- Our first real together
- Our first date
- Our first kiss
- Their dreams
- Their favorite people and why
- Things they loved to do
- Special trips
- First Christmas, Thanksgiving
- Their first birthday with you
- How they celebrated you
- Your first birthday with them
- Things you like doing together
- Your inside jokes
- Special about the proposal
- Special about the wedding
- Special about the honeymoon
- Your first house
- First pet together
- Memories of children with them
- A time they were there for you
- A health issue you went through together
- A spiritual time together

- A time of when you got back together after a fracture in your relationship
- A kiss you'll never forget

That's 25 quick thoughts you already have in your head ready to remember. When you practice being preoccupied, try to actually not just remember the thoughts but allow yourself to feel the feeling of these positive memories together. Remember that lovers, as a general rule, feed the positive and starve the negative thoughts.

 ### Intentional (J)

Do you remember how you could intentionally set it up to look at your lover, see them at work, a certain place or campus? Do you remember how you familiarized yourself with their schedule so you could optimize moments with them?

Do you remember making it a priority for yourself to remember things that were important to them such as specific dates, people and events? Do you remember planning a date for your spouse with such detail that you knew they'd have a good time? Do you remember buying a favorite coffee, tea, chocolate or flower that you knew they would love?

If you're nodding your head yes, yes, yes as I am asking you these questions, you were a lover. You were intentionally loving another with them in mind.

The key word here and a fundamental characteristic is intentionality. A healthy and fit lover-spouse stays intentional over the decades of marriage. A less than fit lover-spouse gives themselves permission to forget what their spouse enjoys, what events or places are important to their lover, and honestly it's more about themselves than being a lover to their spouse.

If you're strong in intentionality, you'll find being a lover very easy, and in most cases, you're already being a pretty good lover-spouse. Intentionality is the spine of being a lover. When we commit to being intentional, we commit to a new path and a new future.

{ *When we commit to being intentional, we commit to a new path and a new future.* }

As a Christian you've heard the prodigal son story (Luke 15: 11-32) preached time and time again. However, I've never heard anyone really experience the power of intentionality in this story.

The Parable of the Lost Son

[11] Jesus continued: "There was a man who had two sons. [12] The younger one said to his father, 'Father, give me my share of the estate.' So, he divided his property between them.

[13] "Not long after that, the younger son got together all he had, set off for a distant country and there squandered his wealth in wild living. [14] After he had spent everything, there was a severe famine in that whole country, and he began to be in need. [15] So he went and hired himself out to a citizen of that country, who sent him to his fields to feed pigs. [16] He longed to fill his stomach with the pods that the pigs were eating, but no one gave him anything.

[17] "When he came to his senses, he said, 'How many of my father's hired servants have food to spare, and here I am starving to death! [18] I will set out and go back to my father and say to him: Father, I have

sinned against heaven and against you.¹⁹ I am no longer worthy to be called your son; make me like one of your hired servants.' ²⁰ So he got up and went to his father.

"But while he was still a long way off, his father saw him and was filled with compassion for him; he ran to his son, threw his arms around him and kissed him.

²¹ "The son said to him, 'Father, I have sinned against heaven and against you. I am no longer worthy to be called your son.'

²² "But the father said to his servants, 'Quick! Bring the best robe and put it on him. Put a ring on his finger and sandals on his feet. ²³ Bring the fattened calf and kill it. Let's have a feast and celebrate. ²⁴ For this son of mine was dead and is alive again; he was lost and is found.' So they began to celebrate.

²⁵ "Meanwhile, the older son was in the field. When he came near the house, he heard music and dancing. ²⁶ So he called one of the servants and asked him what was going on. ²⁷ 'Your brother has come,' he replied, 'and your father has killed the fattened calf because he has him back safe and sound.'

28 "The older brother became angry and refused to go in. So his father went out and pleaded with him. 29 But he answered his father, 'Look! All these years I've been slaving for you and never disobeyed your orders. Yet you never gave me even a young goat so I could celebrate with my friends. 30 But when this son of yours who has squandered your property with prostitutes comes home, you kill the fattened calf for him!'

31 "'My son,' the father said, 'you are always with me, and everything I have is yours. 32 But we had to celebrate and be glad, because this brother of yours was dead and is alive again; he was lost and is found.'"

The story is straightforward. A boy takes his inheritance, moves to a far-off land, and intentionally self-destructs through alcohol and sex. He goes broke.

Then he comes up with a plan of telling his dad he sinned, asking for forgiveness and hoping his dad will hire him on the ranch. However, when he hatched this plan he was in a far-off country. He had to intentionally and consistently walk daily for weeks or months to get back in his father's house.

Intentionality only works if you actually do it. Reading about it isn't doing it. Even planning to do it isn't doing it. Doing it is doing it. Now if for whatever reason you are in the habit of not being an intentional lover toward your spouse, I'd follow the principles of the prodigal.

{ *Intentionality only works if you actually do it. Reading about it isn't doing it.* }

The first part of his plan was to go to his dad and take responsibility. I find as a couple if one or both of you have been irresponsible with being a lover, verbally repenting is very helpful. Unlike the prodigal son I wouldn't try to overcome years or decades of self-absorption, immaturity, inattentiveness, taking the other person for granted, and not being there for them in one conversation.

You could begin to undo some of the damage by writing out the mistakes (sins you made in your relationship with your spouse) and go through this list with them. As you present your list, you could state,

"I need you to forgive me for……" This list could comprise actual things you did, things you didn't do, didn't follow up on, needed to be reminded about repeatedly, attitudes or even just bad ideas.

Taking responsibility also gives you some ideas about creating a plan. You can see where things have to change, and you need to do differently than before.

A couple suggestions I have from my couples work are:

- Write the plan up for yourself.
- Review the plan with your spouse to make sure it achieves what you hope it will.
- Make the goals achievable and measurable. You don't have to do it all in a week but make goals ones you can do and sustain.
- Review your goals with someone of the same gender—a mentor, pastor or cell group leader. This kind of accountability always accelerates your success with such goals.

 ## Creative (C)

A third characteristic of lovers are that they're creative. I don't mean they're crazy artistic creative but creative in how they love their spouse.

They don't stay with the same one way of doing or saying things to their spouse. Over time, as a student of how to love your spouse, you get to know what brings happiness to your spouse.

I remember early in our marriage nothing made Lisa happier than going back to Pennsylvania to see her family. For years we made that 20-hour drive from Texas to Pennsylvania. On Lisa's fiftieth birthday I flew her family to Colorado and surprised her. This brought her real happiness.

I love being a lover. So, I randomly buy cards for Lisa. These aren't just for birthdays or special occasions. These are just simple "I love you" cards so she knows I'm thinking about her. To be creative, I place them in different places—her sink, car, under her pillow, by the blender where she makes her morning smoothie and her office.

If you're already a lover, you've already been creative with your spouse. Keep this going. Not everyone feels good at being creative. Let me share some ideas for those who feel challenged in the area of creativity.

I find creativity is like a muscle—the more you use it, the more it grows and becomes stronger. The less you use creativity, the smaller it becomes in your life.

{ *I find creativity is like a muscle—the more you use it, the more it grows and becomes stronger.* }

Here are a few suggestions if creativity hasn't been your strength. First, for the next 60 days I want you to pray every morning and evening to God your Father and God your Father-in-law about how to be a creative lover to your spouse. I mean this literally. Check off on a calendar for 60 days and see what ideas for being a creative lover come from a variety of sources into your life.

James 1:5 says,

"If any of you lacks wisdom, you should ask God, who gives generously to all without finding fault, and it will be given to you."

Ask God for wisdom. If you're in your servant heart asking God for wisdom, He won't withhold it from you. I'm amazed at the testimonies of how God gives ideas on being a lover when you ask.

Second, ask creative people of the same gender about ways they show love to their spouse or make things special for their spouse. People love sharing these ideas with each other. If you're in a small group like a cell group, ask the leader to bring this topic up for discussion.

Read. There are appropriate blogs, articles, and books available about making marriage fun that you can expose yourself to. These can give you ideas that you can tailor to your spouse who you're trying to love.

If you're willing to ask, you will find answers. Ask God, friends, and the Internet to help you create a masterpiece of being a lover to your spouse.

The following are a few areas you might need to add creativity toward your spouse. Your list likely varies but this is a good start.

1. How you wake up with your spouse—exchange words, touch, or surprise with their drink of choice (i.e., coffee, tea, orange juice, smoothie.)

2. Morning strokes of love

3. Beat them to their chores

4. Get ahead of them with the children

5. Say something different during sex

6. Invite them to lunch

7. Take lunch to them

8. Do a load of laundry for them

9. Fold a load of laundry for them

10. Unload the dishwasher for them for a week.

11. Invite their friends over and leave

12. Get tickets to an event

13. Make a special meal or dessert

14. Invite to sex differently

15. Get a sitter and stay at a hotel

16. Make a gift

17. Buy a class of interest to them and do together

18. Flowers and chocolates

19. Buy the best of something for them

20. Celebrate them on a calendar

21. Have the kids write a card to them

22. Give a massage

23. Whisper to them

24. Go make out somewhere you haven't before

You can decide on these or many other ideas. Here are some areas you might need to be more creative:

1. Chores

2. Parenting

3. Sex

4. Dating

5. Get aways/vacations

6. Food

7. Touch

8. Time to talk

9. Get togethers with friends

 Kinesthetic (K)

One thing that separates the lover relationship from all other relationships is our freedom to physically touch our spouse. Remember when you were dating them? Do you recall how their touch could impact not only your nervous system but "wow" your entire being?

Imagine just the hug or embrace which would send messages of love to you that spoke how much you love, like, and want to be with your spouse. Just writing this makes me want to go touch Lisa.

Touch communicates so much to our spouse. Here is where being extravagant and creative can have a huge impact. Now I know some people don't enjoy touch as much as others or necessarily enjoy it in the same way. Finding the way that they like to be touched, scratched lightly, or massaged can be fun.

Touch is an essential characteristic of being a lover. The touch in the morning affirms that "I love being with you today." The tight embrace, lovers kiss, soft scratch or touch on the back before going to sleep has the same effect.

I know some have concerns about touch because it might lead to sex. However, you can manage that by creating a sexual agreement. A sexual agreement is when a couple agrees on frequency of sexuality together.

So how are you currently doing with touching your spouse? Seriously consider the last 24 hours, the last week, the last month. If your touch was the only measure (and it's not), how will you grade yourself?

Sexual touch is also important as lovers. As a lover -spouse you're the only one privileged to touch their

sacred, sexual areas. Discovering what brings pleasure to your spouse sexually is a privilege. Find the
type of touch which will allow you to be a good sexual lover to your spouse.

Touch is an essential aspect of being a lover-spouse.
I suggest you talk to your spouse on what type of
touch they like:

1. In the morning

2. Coming home

3. In the evening

4. Foreplay

5. During and after sex

6. Bedtime

After this conversation, apply the creativity and intentionality and you have a home run plan for being
a lover-spouse with a great touch!

 Calendar

I'm in social situations on a regular basis just like you are. I'll meet people I already know or meet someone that I would like to get together with to discuss something further.

The "Let's get together" topic comes up and we both think this would be a great idea. They ask when and I say, "I have to check my calendar and then we can schedule it." Once it's on my calendar I consider it put in "stone." They laugh and expect me to pull out my phone.

I see clients during the day up to a certain time but that fluctuates depending on the week. I have a real calendar. I'm talking a paper kind which you use a pen or pencil to write in.

So, we'll usually exchange contact information, or they'll call my office and we'll set a time. One of my amazing administration team will put it on my calendar and the meeting is set, practically in stone.

You might ask why would I have an old-fashioned calendar? First, I was born in that era so I'm comfortable with one. But I also have to be mindful because my clients' names are confidential, and I've never risked that by keeping an electronic calendar.

Now, you might be asking yourself why all this talk about a calendar? Because anything of importance, including dentist, workouts, and hair appointments are all on my calendar. Putting anything on my calendar, even a block that says "write Lover-Spouse book" means it's more likely that I'll then actually do it.

I've seen great success with clients who put dates and other things on their electronic devices to remind them to get things done. When they are purposeful in putting it in their calendar, they're more likely to do it.

As a lover, some of us just intuitively flow in being a lover. It's like a gift. If this has been a challenge for you, then you'll need to be intentional and structure your loverness to manifest toward your spouse. Either way is fine. However, if it's up to this point in your marriage your lover gift lacks flowing, I'd suggest you utilize the ideas in this chapter. Intentionally structuring your lover activities isn't a sign you don't love, it's a sign that you need to organize and structure important things to get them accomplished.

You'll need to be able to use your phone calendar or buy a hard copy calendar and make it your "lover calendar." If your electronic calendar has a reminder alarm feature, definitely use it to help you along the way.

There are definite daily things you might want to do as a lover, so put this on a daily schedule and try to set a specific time so both of you get into a habit of these behaviors. Remember, structure precedes life in God's order.

Suggestions for daily calendar items:

-Do dailies (two feelings, two praises, pray)

-Pray to be a great lover to your spouse

-Keep your word to your spouse

-Write down what you agreed you'd do

-Hug them

-Kiss them

-Check in during the day

-Smile

Now put whatever daily behaviors you want to in your calendar. Then in the space provided, write the date you put these daily things in your calendar.

 Date:_____

Before I go any further on the whole calendar thing, I want to share something with you that can definitely improve your ability to capitalize on your calendar. It will also improve the likelihood that you will actually complete the items on your calendar.

We all know people who write things down and just don't do them. I don't want you to be one of those lover-spouses. I want you to actually cross the finish line and hear "well done."

Any area of life you want to accelerate in will always have a person or people you'll be accountable to. This person is always the same gender. Often this person has genuine affection for you, and depending on the area of life, they might have more expertise in the area than you currently do.

Who could this person be that you could be honest with about your journey to follow through with your lover goals? They don't need to know the specific behaviors but maybe the percentage you've accomplished. You can meet, call or text this person weekly to report the status or your shortcomings the previous week.

Accountability with someone of the same gender raises the bar. Now you've taken this lover thing to a whole other level because you're not only being respectful toward your spouse but finding someone with whom you can bounce ideas off of. As you talk over your situation and ideas with this person, you're much more likely to be a great lover-spouse.

Sadly, Christians will make promises to themselves, even God or their spouse, and be less successful than if they make themselves accountable to someone of the same gender that is NOT a family member.

To add another principle to aid in your calendar success, you can follow a principle of reward or consequence. Give yourself a time period a week, month or quarter. If you're 80 to 90 percent on the lover objectives you put on your calendar, then assign a personal reward for yourself.

However, if you fall below 80 percent, then you can assign a consequence for yourself (i.e., rake leaves, give up something, do more chores or something kind to your spouse that isn't that fun for you).

The consequence acts like a guardrail. If you haven't been a great lover-spouse, your spouse has 100 percent paid the emotional, sexual, romantic cost for your lack of responsibility. You won't ever have to take an aspirin for your spouse's headache because you're not feeling the pain. You might not even believe the pain exists.

I think I've been clear explaining that the ache and pain of not having a lover as a spouse is huge and can create all kinds of havoc in the other spouse's being for sure.

When you set up a consequence, you're saying to yourself and to them, "I'll pay my own bill if I'm an irresponsible lover." When you step up to the plate, like an adult, this can have everlasting change.

You no longer allow them to be in pain, rather you put yourself in pain if you're irresponsible. Now because you're putting pain in the equation, you'll be more likely to be successful with your calendar.

After a few self-inflicted consequences, you'll have time to reflect on your irresponsibility or disregard for your spouse. You can then decide to change your behavior the next week—not just because you love them, but you want to stop having to spank yourself for the same irresponsibility on a regular basis.

Both rewards and consequences work especially well if they're a part of your accountability to another person. This can be really helpful, especially if you've been giving yourself permission to not be a lover to your spouse for years or decades. If your flesh has given you permission or excuses and you traveled the path of irresponsibility unchallenged, you'll especially do well to incorporate all of these ideas. If you have Intimacy Anorexia, I definitely encourage you to use all of these ideas so you can be a great lover-spouse.

Let's go back to the calendar topic. Once you set up your daily ideas for being a great lover-spouse, then you need to move toward some weekly goals. Here you would have to draw upon what has worked in the past with your spouse and maybe come up with some new ideas to do the work.

Weekly suggestions might be:

- A date
- A long walk
- Tea on the back porch
- A love note
- A favorite dessert together
- A back, foot or neck rub
- Watching their favorite show
- Playing their favorite board game
- A sticky note saying "I love you"
- A lover text

Take time to write the weekly goals on your calendar. You might have so many ideas you could spread these over a month or several months. You might only do one or two of these over a week.

Now go to the next week and sprinkle a couple of these in this week. Then go to week three and four and do the same. Once complete, you've done it— you've made your first intentional lover calendar.

Having a lover calendar shows intentionality and greatly improves your chances of being successful. Once you complete your monthly calendar, then you progress to complete the next ninety days or even the whole year.

You and your spouse deserve you to be a rock star lover-spouse. This calendar idea can help you stay on track with being accountable and fostering intentionality so you can actually look back and with a confident sigh and say, "well done."

Appendix

NEW RELEASES

Men Make Men

Dr. Weiss takes the listeners by the hand and step-by-step walks through the creative process God used to make every man into a man of God. This practical teaching on DVD combined with the Men Make Guidebook can revitalize the men in any home or local church. DVD - $29.95   GUIDE BOOK - $11.95

Worthy

This Series is designed for anyone who has struggled with doubting their amazing worth. This insightful and pragmatic journey to worthy is one every believer should experience. You are worth this journey to see what others see - your worth! $29.95

Worthy Exercise & Step book {all in one}

This workbook has been a labor of love. I have seen countless people move from a lifestyle of worthlessness to worthy, and their lives have inspired me to write this. What you have here is a path that anyone can take to get and stay worthy. Follow this path, and you too will make the journey from worthless to worthy, just as others have. $29.95

MARRIAGE

Lover Spouse helps you understand marriage from a Christ-centered perspective. Christian Marriages were designed to be different, passionate, fulfilling, and long-lasting. $13.95

Upgrade Your Sex Life actually teaches you own unique sexual expression that you and your partner are pre-wired to enjoy. $16.95

In these pages you will walk with God as He creates the man, the woman and his masterpiece called marriage. $16.95

This is an eight week marriage training that actually gives you the skills to have a healthy more vibrant marriage. $59.95

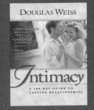

This 100 Day guide can transform couples from any level of intimacy to a lifestyle of satiation with their spouse. $11.99

Dr. Weiss walks you through the creation and maintenance of your marriage. $12.95

By taking ten minutes a day to focus on each other, you can enhance your marriage in ways you'll appreciate for a lifetime. $14.99

This book helps develop faithfulness, patience, forgiveness, service, respect, kindness, and celebration, all of which contribute to an exciting, loving and wonderful relationship. $13.99

In this 12 part DVD series, you will be exposed to tried and true principles to help you learn how to really love a woman. $69.00

INTIMACY ANOREXIA

This hidden addiction is destroying so many marriages today. In your hands is the first antidote for a person or spouse with anorexia to turn the pages on this addiction process. $22.95

This is like therapy in a box. Inside is 100 exercises that have already been proven helpful in treating intimacy anorexia. $39.95

This is the only twelve step workbook just for intimacy anorexia. Each step gives you progress in your healing from intimacy anorexia. $14.95

This book will not only unlock the understanding of intimacy anorexia but you will also hear experiences of spouses who have found themselves married and alone. $14.95

This is the first workbook to offer practical suggestions and techniques to better navigate through recovery from your spouse's Intimacy Anorexia. $39.95

These Steps can further your healing and recovery from your spouse's Intimacy Anorexia. $14.95

This DVD will give you the characteristics, causes and strategies of intimacy anorexia. This DVD also provides solutions for the intimacy anorexic to start their road to recovery. $69.95

This DVD is for the spouse of an intimacy/sexual anorexic. Dr. Weiss will help you to start a journey of recovery from living with a spouse with intimacy anorexia. $49.95

Dr. Weiss has put together the eight reasons why couples might be sexless and married as well as solutions for each reason for sexlessness. $49.95

OTHER RESOURCES

"Born for War" teaches practical tools to defeat these sexual landmines and offers scriptural truths that empower young men to desire successfulness in the war thrust upon them. $29.95

This 2 hour DVD helps single women ages 15-30, to successfully navigate through the season of dating. $29.95

This 2 Disc DVD Series is definitely nothing you have heard before. Dr. Weiss charts new territory as to the why for sexual purity. $29.95

A gift for your daugher as she enters college. Letters to my Daughter includes my daily letters to my daughter during her first year of college. $14.95

Erin discovers she comes from a long line of dragons, dragons who have effectively maintained Earth's balance since the planet's beginning. Will she accept her fate and responsibility? $14.95

Within these pages of this book you will find a tried and true path for recovery from any addiction. Here you will get a biblical understanding to break the strongholds in your life forever. $22.95

This workbook provides tips, biblical principles, techniques, and assignments that Dr. Weiss has given his addicted clients with any addiction for over twenty-five years. $39.95

These steps were derived from a Christian perspective and offer much needed insight and practical wisdom to help you get free and stay free from any addiction. $14.95

This Dvd series includes leadership training and fifty segments that are about 10 minutes in length. Churches of any size can begin a Recovery for Everyone group in their local church. $99.00

CLEAN RESOURCES

Every Christian man is born into a sexual war. The enemy attacks the young, hoping to scar them permanently and leave them ruined. But your past is not enough to keep you from the enduringly clean life you want and deserve. $16.99

This journal is designed to be used in conjunction with the Clean book and the Clean DVD set. This set can be used individually or in a church small group or accountability group. $14.99

This DVD set exposes you to many tried and true spiritual truths with very practical applications. You and your church are about to take an amazing journey towards God's insights for your freedom. $29.99

LUST FREE RESOURCES

Every man can fight for and obtain a lust free lifestyle. Once you know how to stop lust, you will realize how weak lust really can be. God gave you the power to protect those you love from the ravages of lust for the rest of your life! It's time to take it back! $13.95

This DVD series walks you through how every man can fight for and obtain a lust free lifestyle. Once you know how to stop lust, you will realize how weak lust really can be. God gave you the power to protect those you love from the ravages of lust for the rest of your life! It's time to take it back! $23.95

FREE APP!
Download Now!

MEN'S RECOVERY

THE FINAL FREEDOM

DOUGLAS WEISS, PH.D.

This book gives more current information than many professional counselors have today on sexual addiction. $22.95

101 FREEDOM EXERCISES

DOUGLAS WEISS, PH.D.

This workbook will outline the best techniques to help obtain freedom from sexual addiction. $39.95

STEPS TO FREEDOM

DOUGLAS WEISS, PH.D.

This step book is specifically written for the person desiring recovery from sexual addiction. $14.95

Helping Her Heal

Douglas Weiss, Ph.D.

Offers practical tools for hearing her pain, navigating her grief and losses, discovering her expectations of you and the boundaries she may need to heal. $69.95

MARRIAGE AFTER ADDICTION

DOUGLAS WEISS, PH.D.

In this DVD you are intelligently guided through the journey you will experience if addiction is part of your marriage story. $29.95

After Infidelity

Douglas Weiss Ph.D.

Helps identify key points about the whys of infidelity, the types of cheaters, and how to start walking toward a healthy marriage. $49.95

6 TYPES OF SEX ADDICTS

DOUGLAS WEISS, PH.D.

This CD will give you more information than most therapists have on sexual addiction. You will be able to finally know how you became a sexual addict and identify why you might still be relapsing. $29.95

TREATMENTS FOR THE 6 TYPES OF SEX ADDICTS

DOUGLAS WEISS, PH.D.

Once you know the type of sex addict you are, Dr. Doug outlines the same treatment plan you would receive in an individual session. $29.95

Addict to Addict
Douglas Weiss, Ph.D.

This amazing DVD has 8 addicts telling their stories through directed questions. These individuals address key issues along with their journey through recovery. $19.95

WOMEN'S RECOVERY

This book offers the readers hope, along with a plan for recovery. Any woman who is a partner of a sex addict will find this book a necessity for her journey toward healing. $14.95

This is like therapy in a box for women who want to walk through the residual effects of being in a relationship with a sex addict. $39.95

This is an interactive workbook that allows the partners of sex addicts to gain insight and strength through working the Twelve Steps. $14.95

This DVD provides a clear path to processing your desire for safety and creates a roadmap to reclaim safety regardless of your partner or spouse's choices. $29.95

This DVD is for every woman who has experienced the pain of their partner's sex addiction or intimacy anorexia and feels stuck, confused, frustrated and unable to move on.$29.00

This DVD set helps women accept this immature reality and gives them practical ways to navigate their husband's re-maturing process if he chooses recovery. $49.99

Your pain and betrayal are real and are addressed in this DVD series. You deserve the best answer to your questions and in just under 2 hours you can have them answered for you. $69.95

In this DVD set Dr. Weiss will expose the viewer to specific reasons as to why men lie and helpful strategies to end the lying. $44.95

This CD series addresses all three aspects of a couple recovering from the impacts of sexual addiction. $19.95

A·A·S·A·T

American Association for Sex Addiction Therapy

Cost: $795

Both male and female clinicians are desiring to counsel sexually addictive behaviors more than ever. You can be prepared! Forty-eight hours of topics related to sexual addiction treatment are covered in this training including:

- The Six Types of Sex Addicts
- Sex and Recovery
- Case Assessment
- Behavior Treatment Plans for each type

- Neurological Understanding
- Relapse Strategies
- Comorbidity Issues
- Intimacy Anorexia

Cost: $595

With this AASAT training, you will gain proven clinical insight into treating the issues facing partners of sex addicts. You can be prepared! Over thirty hours of topics related to partners treatment are covered in this training, including:

- Partner Model
- Anger
- Partners as Intimacy Anorexics
- Separation

- Partner Grief
- Boundaries
- Reactive Intimacy Anorexia
- Polygraph Questions

Cost: $695

This is the only available training to become certified to treat Intimacy Anorexia. Dr. Weiss developed this training program utilizing his own, proven methodology and modality as well as his clinical application for treatment.

This growing issue of Intimacy Anorexia will need your competent help in your community. Now, you can be prepared to identify it and treat it. In this training you'll cover topics like:

- Identifying Intimacy Anorexia
- Comorbid Issues
- Relapse Strategies
- Characteristics of Intimacy Anorexia

- Causes of Intimacy Anorexia
- Treatment Plan
- Marital Treatment
- Sexual Recovery Issues

For More Information:
Call 719.330.2425 or visit www.aasat.org

COUNSELING

"Without the intensive, my marriage would have ended and I would not have known why. Now I am happier than ever and my marriage is bonded permanently."

Counseling Sessions

Couples are helped through critical phases of disclosure moving into the process of recovery, and rebuilding trust in relationships. We have helped many couples rebuild their relationship and grasp and implement the necessary skills for an intimate relationship.

Individual counseling offers a personal treatment plan for successful healing in your life. In just one session a counselor can help you understand how you became stuck and how to move toward freedom.

Partners of sex addicts need an advocate. Feelings of fear, hurt, anger, betrayal, and grief require a compassionate, effective response. We provide that expert guidance and direction. We have helped many partners heal through sessions that get them answers to their many questions including: "How can I trust him again?"

A counseling session today can begin your personal journey toward healing.

3 and 5 Day Intensives

in Colorado Springs, Colorado are available for the following issues:

* Sexual Addiction
* Marriage
* Pastors
* Partners of Sexual Addicts
* Intimacy Anorexia
* Victims of Sexual Abuse
* Adult Children of Sex Addicts
* Teenage Children of Sex Addicts
* Teens

Attendees of Intensives will receive:

* Personal attention from counselors who specialize in your area of need

* An understanding of how the addiction /anorexia and its consequences came into being

* Three counseling sessions daily

* Daily assignments to increase the productiveness of these daily sessions

* Individuals get effective counseling to recover from the effects of sexual addiction, abuse and intimacy anorexia.

* Addiction, abuse, anorexia issues are thoroughly addressed for couples and individuals. This includes the effects on the partner or family members of the addict, and how to rebuild intimacy toward a stronger relationship.

CONFERENCES

What an incredible way to deliver such a sensitive, "hush hush" topic!! Thank you from the bottom of my heart. I really enjoyed tonight's conference. Today will count as the first day of my sexual sobriety.

CLEAN
is a powerful men's conference equipping men to join the battle to maintain sexual purity. In this conference, men will be given tools and biblical principles so they can get started immediately.

PURITY
Mixed audiences can be impacted by *Successfully Single*, as well as *Born for War* for Male Teens and *Princes take Longer than Frogs* for Female Teens to help motivate them to fight for their sexual purity.

MEN
The *Lust Free Living* or *Sex, Men & God* conferences is where men experience great personal growth and understanding into their sexuality and how to be lust free...where other speakers rarely go. *How to Really Love a Woman* is really practical training for the men in your church.

COUPLES
attending the *Servant Marriage, Intimacy, 10 Minute Marriage* or *The 7 Love Agreements* Conference discover how to discuss their desires, learn the importance of marital dating, how to connect emotionally, how to let go of your past and much more.

WOMEN
How to Really Love a Man and *Best Sex for Women* are great inspiring and practical teachings for the women in your church.

For additional conference information, including available dates, please call our office at 719-278-3708, visit our website at www.drdougweiss.org or you may also email us at lisa@drdougweiss.com